GIT intermediate
Know abstractions you use.

Jacek Drąg

GIT intermediate

Know abstractions you use.

ISBN: 979-8-8662-8620-1
Independently published

To my wife

Table of Contents

Preface

While working with Git, graphical tools can be used. They make some things easier and are especially useful for reviewing history and conflicts resolving.

In this book we will concentrate on how to develop the repository, or in other words — how to grow *the commit graph*. *Command line* will be used as the most powerful tool suitable for this purpose, specifically *bash* will be used. Windows users often use **git bash** [https://gitforwindows.org/] or **WSL** [https://learn.microsoft.com/en-us/windows/wsl/install] (Windows Subsystem for Linux) anyway.

In this book you will learn about

- Abstractions used by Git.
- The majority of high-level commands — their most common and some more interesting use cases.
- A few low-level commands.
- How to work locally and remotely.

You will also learn to understand a bit what Git says when executing commands. Git is talkative yet often not easy to understand. Talkative in such sense that when you ask it to execute a command not only will it execute the command, but it also will:

- comment on what's happening,
- give you some clues,
- report why something has failed.

Part I: Git locally

If you are already using Git, you can go straight to *The stupid content tracker* and come back to configuration chapter when needed. You only need to apply configuration from *Configuration used in this book*, so that the examples from the book could work.

1. Configuration

1.1. Installation

Windows

> Use ***git-bash*** [https://git-scm.com/downloads] or ***WSL*** [https://learn.microsoft.com/en-us/windows/wsl/install]. This book uses *bash*.

Linux, Mac OS

> No comment.

It is worth looking online and configuring:

- Command completion.
- Prompt coloring.

1.2. `git config` — configuration

Documentation: ***git config*** [https://git-scm.com/docs/git-config]

To see detailed information on Git configuration one can type:

```
git config
```

```
git help config
```

1.2.1. Local and global configuration

The values of each configuration option can be set on several levels. Two most often used are:

local (default)   For a given repository. Usually saved in `.git/config` file.

global   For a given user. Usually saved in `~/.gitconfig` file.

Some other possibility is:

system   For all users of the computer.

1.2.2. Structure of the configuration file

Configuration options are grouped into sections and subsections.

The option names are as follows <section>.<key>, or <section>.<subsection>.<key> in case of having subsection.

Exemplary section color *and subsection* color.status *from* ~/.gitconfig

```
[color]
        status = always
        branch = auto
        ui = always
[color "status"]
        added = green
        changed = yellow
        untracked = red
```


1.2.3. Displaying values

To display the configuration one can type:

```
git config [--local | --global] [--show-origin] (-l | --list)
```

--show-origin causes the name of the value's source file to be displayed

```
git config --show-origin -l
```

The value of a specific option can be also displayed:

```
git config [--local | --global] [--show-origin] --get <name>
```


1.2.4. Setting values

The values are most often set with the command:

```
git config [--local | --global] <name> <value>
```

But the config file can be also edited just by hand.

1.2.5. Command aliases

The `alias` section allows user to create their own commands, e.g. shortcuts for commands.

```
git config --global alias.st status
git st
git config --global alias.sst 'status --short'
git sst
```

The exclamation mark (!) has a special meaning. It allows a shell script to be run instead of a Git command.

Stupid example

```
git config alias.ll '! ls -l'
git ll
```

1.2.6. Deleting the values

A value can be deleted with `--unset` option:

```
git config [--local | --global] --unset <name>
```

Small experiment

```
git config --get foo.bar
git config foo.bar baz
git config --get foo.bar
git config --unset foo.bar
git config --get foo.bar
```

1.3. Minimal configuration

It is necessary to introduce yourself to Git before working with it. It can be done this way:

```
git config --global user.name "My Name"
git config --global user.email me@email.com
```

It is convenient to set those values globally (as above). It can be always overridden with `--local` option for any particular repository.

1.4. Often used options

- core.editor

vi is the default editor.

1.5. Rarely used options

Many default settings/behaviours can be configured. E.g. the default name of a remote repository is *origin*. It can be changed (from version 2.30.0) by setting the value of `clone.defaultRemoteName` option.

Most options can be found in the ***documentation** [https://git-scm.com/docs/git-config#_variables]*.

1.6. Configuration used in this book

The commands used in this book will often assume that the configuration shown below has been applied.

Adding slog (simple log) command

```
git config --global alias.slog "log -n 30 --graph --pretty=format:'%C(yellow)%h%Creset
%Cgreen%ad%Creset %C(blue bold)%<(10,trunc)%an%Creset %s%C(auto)%d%Creset' --date=format:'%Y-%m
-%d %H:%M'"
```

Adding alog (all log) command

```
git config --global alias.alog "log -n 30 --graph --pretty=format:'%C(yellow)%h%Creset
%Cgreen%ad%Creset %C(blue bold)%<(10,trunc)%an%Creset %s%C(auto)%d%Creset' --date=format:'%Y-%m
-%d %H:%M' --all"
```

Status coloring

```
git config --global color.status.added green
git config --global color.status.changed yellow
git config --global color.status.untracked red
```

Some command shortcuts

```
git config --global alias.st status
git config --global alias.sst 'status --short'
```

2. Local repository

2.1. `git` — the stupid content tracker

Documentation: **_git_** [https://git-scm.com/docs/git]

At the very beginning, let's see what Git says about itself:

Linux

```
man git
```

Windows

```
git help git
```

You should see something like this:

```
NAME
        git - the stupid content tracker

(...)

DESCRIPTION
        Git is a fast, scalable, distributed revision control system with an unusually rich
command set that provides both high-level operations and full access to internals.

(...)

        After you mastered the basic concepts, you can come back to this page to learn what
commands Git offers.
```

As mentioned, you will learn:

- *basic concepts*
- *commands*
  - a lot of *high-level* (called also *porcelain*)
  - a few *low-level* (called also *plumbing*)

Usually commands take many parameters. Some of the parameters are taken by many commands.

Parameters taken by many commands

(-n | --dry-run)	Only show what the command would do.
(-v | --verbose)	More talkative version.
(-q | --quiet)	Quiet version.
[--] [\<spec>...]	Commands operating on files/paths can have many of them specified. Often it's useful to separate other parameters from the files/paths specifications. The parameters go before double dash (`--`), the files/paths go after it. This can help to avoid ambiguity (e.g. whether `foo` should be treated as a file or a branch name).

2.1.1. Tracking the history of changes — the history of commits

Git is used to track the history of changes of a given directory. Most often, it will be a directory containing some IT project. But it can contain also master's thesis, a dissertation, or anything else. Simply put, when you have important files in a directory, which history of changes is important to you, you can use Git. Most likely it will be the best choice!

We will call such a directory a *project* because it usually contains a certain 'project'.

Git tracks the content of the project and allows:

- To review its history of changes.
- To restore the content of the project from a chosen saved state.

However, it does not track this content on its own. It just saves those project states — snapshots of the project — that the user has deemed important and **explicitly** asked Git to save them. Changes cannot be restored from **any** moment in time but only from any of the **saved** states (the snapshots).

More specifically, working with Git goes the way:

- The user adds, edits and deletes files in the project (i.e. in the tracked directory).
- When they decide that the current state of the project should be saved (the whole project or only some files):
    ◦ They instruct Git which files should be saved in their current state.
    ◦ They order Git to save the state.
      Specifying a commit message — a description of significant changes made since the previous saved state. This message is later useful when reviewing the history.

An analogy can be seen with making and committing changes to relational database. First, one makes changes to the database (perhaps in several steps), then they commit the changed state of the database. Before committing, it is possible to roll back the changes.

Such a saved project state is called *a Git commit*. What is important: Git saves as its commits the entire project snapshots. Not the changes made since the previous snapshot had been saved, or anything else. Just a snapshot.

Thus, a commit is a saved snapshot of the **whole content** of the project. It may not seem important whether Git saves snapshots or just the differences between the previous content and the current one. Yet it is important, what will become apparent in time.

Git holds the history of commits, i.e. snapshots of the **whole content** of the project (the tracked directory). The snapshots to be saved have to be explicitly pointed out by the user.

2.1.2. Content of the project

Let's repeat: Git tracks the content of its project, where a project is just a certain directory on the disk.

By project content, Git means:

- The structure of its directories.
- The files in those directories.

Git considers that the **real content** lays in the files, as a consequence it is completely uninterested in empty directories.

Thus, if you create an empty directory, e.g. foo, or even a directory with a subdirectory, e.g. foo/bar, but you put **no** file there, Git will ignore such a directory — it will not save it in any commit. It doesn't even have such a possibility! To illustrate this behaviour, let's conduct a small experiment.

Small experiment

```
mkdir experiment1
cd experiment1
git init ①
mkdir -p foo/bar ②
git status ③
git add foo ④
git status ⑤
git commit -m"Do commit anyway" ⑥
touch foo/bar/x.txt ⑦
git status ⑧
git add foo ⑨
git status ⑩
git commit -m"Do commit, second try" ⑪
git slog ⑫
git show ⑬
```

① Initializing directory `experiment1` as a Git project (in other words: creating a repository)

② Creating a directory with a subdirectory

③ Checking that Git does not notice the created directories

④ Attempting to add the directory to the commit being prepared

⑤ Checking that nothing has changed

⑥ Attempting to create the first commit

⑦ Adding a file

⑧ Checking if anything has changed

⑨ Adding the `foo` directory (along with its subdirectories) to the commit being prepared

⑩ Checking if anything has changed

⑪ Creating the commit

⑫ Displaying the (one-element) history of commits

⑬ Displaying the commit

 Git **does not** save empty directories. A directory (itself or any of its subdirectories) **must** contain a file to be eligible for saving. The file itself can be empty.

2.1.3. Text files, binary files

Git is best suited for tracking text files such as source code, documentation in latex, adoc, md formats. However, if in your project you use binary files (e.g. office files, images, etc.), you can use Git as well.

A frequently raised problem is the volume of a repository containing binary files. They are large and compress poorly as they are already compressed. Let's assume, that you have a 100M file and 10 versions of the file, which means you need 1G of disk space. This may seem like a lot, but if you really want to have these 10 versions saved, then after all, space for them has to be found.

 Git can be used with binary files, although reasonably.

2.2. The `.git` directory — the Git repository

A question could be asked: Since Git stores the project history, it has to store this history **somewhere**. Where is it?

Small experiment

```
mkdir experiment2
cd experiment2
git init ①
ls -al
```

```
tree .git ②
```

① Git probably answered:
   ```
   Initialized empty Git repository in <somepath>/experiment2/.git/.
   ```

② Several files and subdirectories were created in the .git directory.
   Some of those will be discussed in next chapters. Caution: Windows users need to use
   `tree.com .git`.

So, we suspect that Git stores the project history in the .git subdirectory. This is the case indeed.
Let's note some implications of this fact:

- Deleting this directory deletes **the whole** project history.

- Copying this directory means making a backup of **the whole** project history. Primitive
  perhaps, but it works!

- To find out if the current directory is tracked by Git (if it is a Git project in our
  nomenclature), all you need to do is to check whether it contains the .git subdirectory or
  not.
  This is not entirely true, because .git must contain certain components to be a Git
  repository. But if the directory was created by Git, it will contain all the necessary
  components (see tree .git command above). And would any normal person create a
  directory named *.git* manually?

Hm. Let's do it!

Small experiment

```
mkdir experiment3
cd experiment3
mkdir .git
mkdir .git/objects
mkdir .git/refs
echo "ref: refs/heads/master" > .git/HEAD
tree .git
git status
```

Hm, it doesn't take much for Git to recognize the .git directory as its repository.

Small experiment continued

```
touch a.txt
git add a.txt
git commit -m"init repo"
tree .git
cat .git/HEAD
cat .git/refs/heads/master
```

HEAD and the files with refs/heads and refs/objects are entities to be discussed in the following chapters.

The .git directory itself is a Git repository, i.e. everything Git knows about the project, in particular the whole project history. It is so-called a local repository. Local — because we use it as if it was on a local drive.

If you are working alone, and you just want to store project history locally, then such a local repository is all you need. However, cooperation with someone else, sharing the work done, is a common case. Technically, such sharing is transferring saved snapshots of the project between several repositories. I.e. you can download (git fetch) to you local repository snapshots saved by colleagues in their repositories (local from their point of view, remote from yours) and send them (git push) the changes saved in your local repository (remote from their point of view).

> The Git repository is a place where Git stores everything it needs to track the project. In particular, repository stores the whole history of the project. Normally, this repository is the .git subdirectory, which is a subdirectory of the directory being tracked.

2.3. Objects in repository, commit graph, content-addressable map

2.3.1. Commit as an object

You already know that each commit stores a snapshot of the project. In addition, each commit stores some other important information. Strictly speaking, each commit stores the following data:

- the snapshot of the project
- the *commit message*, which is a message given during the commit creation
- the *parent commits* list
- the name and email of the *author*
- the creation time
- the name and email of the *committer*
- the committing time

A commit storing the content described above, is considered by Git as a kind of object. For each of its objects, Git assigns its identifier. Let's try to observe the identifier and the components of a commit object.

Small experiment

```
mkdir experiment4
cd experiment4
git init
```

```
touch a.txt
git add a.txt
git commit -m"init repo"
touch b.txt
git add b.txt
git commit -m"second commit"
```

Displaying information about current commit

```
git show --name-only
```

Text displayed

```
commit a2156780bfe1b5e0803f1b02dc8a3862dc3c1f72 (HEAD -> master)
Author: Jacek Drag <jacadrag@gmail.com>
Date:   Thu Aug 25 16:44:20 2022 +0200

    second commit

b.txt
```

You can see, among others, the commit identifier (a string of letters and numbers).

or

Displaying information about commit, as a Git object

```
git cat-file -p HEAD
```

Text displayed

```
tree 2bdf04adb23d2b40b6085efb230856e5e2a775b7
parent e9796c1ddf8508bf95da41c6118b9537ebef1b82
author Jacek Drag <jacadrag@gmail.com> 1661438660 +0200
committer Jacek Drag <jacadrag@gmail.com> 1661438660 +0200

second commit
```

Indeed, you can see the individual components of the commit:

tree   Under this mysterious name *tree / tree object* content of the project
                            (the snapshot) is stored.

parent	The identifier of the parent commit (the list of parents is one-element).
author	The author with timestamp.
committer	The committer with timestamp. The same as the **author**.
commit message	The commit message.

Let's go a step further and display the project content stored in the commit. I.e. the content of commit's tree.

Displaying the tree content

```
git cat-file -p HEAD^{tree}
```

```
100644 blob e69de29bb2d1d6434b8b29ae775ad8c2e48c5391    a.txt
100644 blob e69de29bb2d1d6434b8b29ae775ad8c2e48c5391    b.txt
```

Hm:

- some new identifiers, in fact one new identifier repeated twice
- something called *blob*
- file names

Ok, the file names correspond to those created on the disk. It seems to make sense.
But *blob*? Blob is — in some simplification — the content of a file. In this case, both files contain the same content. Specifically, they are empty. e69de29bb2d1d6434b8b29ae775ad8c2e48c5391 is the identifier of the empty file's content.

Commit is an object created with `git commit` command. Each commit consists of five elements:

- the snapshot of the project
- the commit message — provided by the user when committing
- the list of parents (each parent from the list is also a commit)
- the information about the author along with authoring timestamp
- the information about committer along with commit creation timestamp

2.3.2. Commit graph

Let's get a closer look at this.

We can skip the committer and theirs timestamp at the moment (git show command also considered it appropriate) because they will usually be identical to the author's data. The fact that this data may be significantly different from the author's data will be discussed later.

On the other hand, the parents list is extremely important. It sets *being a parent* relationship between commits pairs. Furthermore, this relationship induces the relationships of *being an ancestor* and *being a descendant*.

 We say, that commit **A** is a parent of commit **B**, if commit **A** can be found on the parents list of commit **B**.

The intention is clear: Let's say the last created commit is **A**. You make changes to the project and commit it, resulting in commit **B** creation. In some — pretty clear sense — commit **A** precedes (directly) commit **B** in the history of changes/development of the project. Creating (on your command) commit **B**, Git will automatically add commit **A** to the commit **B** parents list. Moreover, this list will be one-element. So, one could say that the current commit automatically becomes (the only) parent of the new commit.

Parents list:

- Most often is one-element.
- Is empty for only one commit in the repository. I.e. for the first created commit (the root). Git was unable to deduce any parent for it.
  Alright — it is possible to create more of such commits, but normally there is just one such a commit.
- If it has two or more elements, this commit is called a *merge commit*.
  However, the lists that has more than two elements are very rare.

 Commits along with relationship of being a parent create a graph[1], more precisely, an acyclic directed graph (*directed acyclic graph*, abbreviated as *DAG*).

2.3.3. Commit ID, map of objects (database)

One could say, that being DAG is a property of the Git repository — interesting and very important. How Git stores its objects is also interesting and very important.

For each commit, Git calculates its *commit ID*. That is value of the SHA-1[2] function calculated for some textual representation of the commit. This representation is more or less like the one you saw with git cat-file -p HEAD command. Commit ID is also often called a *hash*.

Commit is one of the four (and only four!) kinds of objects stored by Git.

For the three others Git computes theirs SHA-1 as well. All objects are stored in a map — mapping hashes of the objects to the objects themselves:

```
<SHA-1 of the object> → <the object on which SHA-1 was calculated>
```

This technique is called content-addressing: the key under which a value is stored is calculated based on this value.

Git objects are very often referenced by their ID (SHA-1 hash). You saw this with `git cat-file` and `git show` commands.

The SHA-1 value consists of 40 characters.

It can be easily seen that this solution is incorrect! Indeed: there are infinitely many potential commits, so **some different** commits must have **the same** commit ID, and consequently it is impossible to keep all of them in the same map, because only one object can be kept under one key.

In practice however, the SHA-1 function is good enough hash function. Therefore, one can assume that there is no such danger. Often 5-6 characters long prefix uniquely identifies the entire key (and therefore the entire object!) within the given repository. While 12 characters long prefix is currently considered secure — unique within all existing repositories.
Therefore:
For any SHA-1 prefix (let's say the first 8 characters) of any object in the map, there will most likely be **exactly one key** with this prefix in the map, and this is the key to map the object. This is very convenient, because it allows to write:

```
git show 82e6777a
```

instead of:

```
git show 82e6777acc5d28eb0888f8917f64ebc47f756548
```

If in command, where Git expects SHA-1, one passes not the entire SHA-1 value but only a prefix of this SHA-1, Git checks whether the prefix uniquely identifies some SHA-1 key from the map. If yes then it uses that SHA-1. It complains if not. In practice, a prefix consisting of about 6 characters can be used. It can also happen that the given argument is not a prefix of any key but some name (e.g. HEAD). Git can usually handle this and knows whether it is a special name or an SHA-1 hash, and complains if the name passed happens to be also a prefix of some hash.

```
git cat-file HEAD
```

Git objects are stored in a content-addressable map.

2.3.4. Other types of objects

Apart from commits, Git only stores three other kinds of objects:

trees / tree objects	representations of directories
blobs	(compressed) file contents
annotated tags	containing:

- the tag's name
- commit ID of the annotated commit
- message (similar to commit message)
- author with timestamp (similar to commit author)

As with commits, Git calculates SHA-1 hash for each object and puts the object into the map.

Besides annotated tags, which are objects, there are also *lightweight tags*, which are not objects but *refs*.

Git objects can be displayed with ***cat-file*** [https://git-scm.com/docs/git-cat-file] command. The command has several forms, we will use:

```
git cat-file <type-or-option> <object-expression>
```

<type>'s possible values:

- commit
- tree
- blob

<option>'s possible values:

-p   pretty-print — recognizes the type of object and displays the recognized object

-t   displays the type of the object instead of its content

-s   displays the size of the object instead of its content

-e   checks if the object exists

<object expression> is described in ***Addressing expressions***.

Small experiment

```
mkdir experiment5
cd experiment5
git init
touch README.txt
git add README.txt
git commit -m"Initialize repo"
git show --name-only
git cat-file -p HEAD
git cat-file -p HEAD^{tree}
```

Git stores four kinds of objects only:

- commits
- trees — directories (files and subdirectories lists)
- blobs — files contents
- annotated tags — to annotate selected commits

2.3.5. Immutability of commits and commit graph

Commits are immutable, in particular commits parents list cannot be changed. As a result, once created, no part of the graph can change. But the graph can grow! However, Git can remove commits (see **Garbage collection**) from the repository, but only no longer accessible ones. So one can say that the removed commits never existed.

Once created commit **never** changes.

2.3.6. The dualism — graph vs database

Logically, a repository is a commit graph, in which some nodes (commits) are decorated with labels (refs). Sometimes, however, it is more important that this graph is stored in the repository in the form of a database — content-addressable map.

For example, let's say a colleague is working on the same project as you. They did something interesting, and you want to download the effects of their work. It means that there are new commits, trees, blobs created in their database, and you want to put the objects into your local database. While fetching Git first checks which keys (those 40-character SHA-1) are missing in your database, and then it fetches all these keys along with the corresponding objects and puts it all into your local database. And that's it, job's done!

Now you want to see changes your colleague made (the commits they added). So you look at the graph — how it has changed. Specifically, how it has grown up.

Cooperation between the local repository and the remote ones is basically sending objects (both ways). What, after sending and adding to the map, makes the commits graph grow.

Awesome!

2.3.7. *Merge commits*

One could notice that if all commits (except the starting one, the root) have only one parent, the graph is not an interesting one. It is a bamboo.

Commits with a few-element list of parents (usually two), are called *merge commits*, and it is their existence that makes the graph interesting. But interesting means complicated. Personally, I prefer simple graphs — mostly bamboos, but we will come to that.

2.4. *Refs* — normal and symbolic, branches

Now we know that Git repository is represented by directed, acyclic commit graph. Next goal is to:

- Expand (grow) the graph by creating new commits.
- Traverse the graph.

A *ref* points to a commit. (For programmers: analogy to the pointers is accurate). Refs are constantly used during everyday work. Ref, in opposite to commit, **can** change — first pointing to commit **A**, later to commit **B**.

There are two kinds of refs:

- *Normal ref* points to a commit. It just stores a commit ID.
- *Symbolic ref* points to another ref. It stores the name of the ref.

Most refs are stored in subdirectories of .git/refs directory. Some special refs (used for current work) are stored directly in .git directory.

One of the most important kind of refs is *branch*. By default, master is the first branch created during initialization of the repository.

Facility of creating, merging and distributed sharing branches is one of the fundamental Git features, that makes Git so powerful *distributed version control system* (*DVCS*).

Refs are used for effective dealing with the commit graph.

They can point directly to commits (*normal refs*) or to another refs (*symbolic refs*).

Branches are normal refs, so branches point to commits. These commits are called *tips of the branches* (from a given moment).

2.4.1. The most important ref — *HEAD*

HEAD is the most important ref. Git repository cannot exist without HEAD. Working with Git always means using HEAD, even if unconsciously.

Usually HEAD is a symbolic ref (it points to a branch. However, that is not always the case. When HEAD isn't a symbolic ref, you are in *detached HEAD* state (which will be discussed soon). Although some people like to work in detached HEAD state, it isn't a typical approach. In fact, if you work in detached HEAD state, Git will most likely be reminding you about it, and it will ask you to switch to the more typical state, which is the one with HEAD pointing to some branch.

HEAD

- Is stored in `.git/HEAD` file.
- Typically, if the repository is empty (no commits have been created), it points to the yet not existing branch `master`.
- During commit:
    - At first, the commit to which HEAD is pointing to (most likely — as a symbolic ref — indirectly), becomes the parent of the commit **being created**. That means, it is written to the one-element parents list of the new-created commit.
    - After saving the new-**created** commit in the repository (map of objects), HEAD starts to point to this new commit. Normally it means, that the branch pointed by HEAD changes. In detached HEAD state however, this means that HEAD itself changes.

 Git cannot function without **HEAD**. During committing, the commit pointed by HEAD becomes the only parent of the new-created commit.

2.4.2. A couple of experiments with refs and HEAD

Assuming that Git:

- Stores objects in `.git/objects` directory.
- Stores refs in `.git/refs` directory.
- Must have HEAD, which is stored in `.git/HEAD` file.

Let's try to create a Git repository manually.

Manual, minimalistic `git init`

```
mkdir experiment6
cd experiment6
mkdir -p .git/objects
mkdir -p .git/refs
echo 'ref: refs/heads/master' > .git/HEAD
git status
```

It works!

Let's keep going!

```
git symbolic-ref HEAD ①
git rev-parse HEAD ②
git commit --allow-empty -m"init repo"
touch y.txt
git add y.txt
git rev-parse HEAD ③
git commit -m"Committed when HEAD was $(git rev-parse HEAD)."
git rev-parse HEAD ④
git cat-file commit HEAD ⑤
```

① HEAD is a symbolic ref pointing to the branch master (we'll talk about heads in a while).

② HEAD is not pointing to any commit yet. There are no commits in the repository for now.

③ HEAD value before committing.

④ HEAD value after committing.

⑤ The parent of the new commit is the previous HEAD's value.

2.4.3. Heads as tips of the branches and branches

As mentioned before, the idea of branches is one of the most important concepts that makes Git so powerful.

What are those branches?
Technically, they are just (normal) refs, living in the .git/refs/heads directory.
Why not in .git/refs/branches though?!
The answer is:

Technically, a branch is just a ref. However, to realize what the term 'branch' really means, we have to consider the ref as a **tip of the branch**. The branch is defined by its tip and the parent relationship.
So, we can see the 'branch' as a subgraph: consisting of its tip itself and all commits reachable by parent relationship.

Now, reversing the order, we can see the branch as something that starts at the first commit (the root) of the repository and expands, possibly diverging and merging, until it finally reaches its tip — the current commit.
Moreover, that branch still can grow — it's as easy as creating a new commit on its tip (i.e. when HEAD is pointing to the tip).

If we take this point of view, our refs will indeed be pointing to the **tips** of the branches. Therefore, refs/heads may be technically more accurate location.

During work, HEAD usually points to the 'current' branch (its tip), e.g. .git/refs/heads/master. It allows the branch to grow by creating a new commit on the tip of the branch.

Useful checks

```
git symbolic-ref HEAD ①
git rev-parse refs/heads/master ②
git rev-parse HEAD ③
```

① HEAD is a symbolic ref, it points to some branch, e.g. refs/heads/master.

② refs/heads/master is a normal ref, which points to some commit — the tip of the branch (its head).

③ HEAD indirectly points to the same commit as refs/heads/master
Yeah — if HEAD points to refs/heads/master, what other commit could it indirectly point to?

2.4.4. Naming conventions

Name of a branch can include slashes (/). Using it makes the names look like file paths or contained in namespaces. It might be a good idea to decide on some convention for big projects. E.g. dividing branches into some categories:

- feature/* from short-lived branches intended to develop features,
- user/<user>/* for individual programmers, so that they can have their own branches without polluting the "general namespace",

or anything else that seems useful.

2.4.5. Useful commands

git branch	Display local branches.
git branch -vv	Display branches taking into account tracking info.
git branch --all	Display local and tracking branches.
git show-ref	Display refs.
git symbolic-ref \<name\>	Display which ref \<name\> is pointing to.

2.4.6. Lightweight tags

Another kind of refs are lightweight tags. They are normal refs used to (temporary) tag commits. To tag commits permanently *annotated tags* should be used, which are not refs but Git objects (see **Git objects**).

[1] A graph consists of nodes and edges, i.e. connections between two selected nodes. In a directed graph, each edge has a direction. For example, you can imagine a graph as cities on a map with roads (non-intersecting, intersections are forbidden) connecting some pairs of the cities. If the roads are one-way, you are dealing with a directed graph. A graph is acyclic when it has no cycles. That means, starting from any node, driving along the edges one can never go back to the starting node. So one can't make a closed loop.

[2] *hash function / cryptographic hash function* is a concept from, let's say, math/cryptography. It should work like this: for any change of its argument it produces a completely different result. E.g.
SHA-1(abcdefgh) = 425af12a0743502b322e93a015bcf868e324d56a
SHA-1(abcdefgH) = ee09d684957fc46acc40ee017f24f4be6ef5a2a8

3. Playing with graph

3.1. Some technical preparations

It's needed to apply some configuration to enable the simple playing with the graph.
Caution: the configuration commands are long. They have to be executed as whole lines without breaking them.

Preparation for playing with "the stupid content tracker":

```
git config --global alias.stupid-commit '!f() { git commit --allow-empty -m"$1"; }; f'
git config --global alias.stupid-merge '!f() { git merge --no-ff $1 -m"merging $1"; }; f'
git config --global alias.stupid-octopus '!f() { git merge --no-ff -m"merging $@" $@; }; f'
git config --global alias.stupid-amend 'commit --allow-empty --amend -m'
git config --global alias.stupid-cherry-pick 'cherry-pick --allow-empty'
git config --global alias.stupid-reset-to-root '!f() { git checkout master && git reset --hard
$(git rev-list --max-parents=0 HEAD) && git branch | grep -v master | xargs git branch -D; }; f'
git config --global alias.stupid-rebase '!f() { if [ -z "$3" ]; then echo "I need 3 commits";
else git rebase -q --force-rebase --keep-empty --onto $1 $2 $3; fi; }; f'
git config --global alias.stupid-interactive-rebase '!f() { if [ -z "$3" ]; then echo "I need 3
commits"; else git rebase -i -q --force-rebase --keep-empty --onto $1 $2 $3; fi; }; f'
```

I suggest to use the `git alog` command after each commit creation, or even more often, to see how the commit graph has changed.

Sample line

```
* 45229e0 2021-12-29 15:40 Jacek Drag a (HEAD -> b1, b2)
```

means:

- Asterisk (*) means commit. Together with additional lines shows the graph structure.
- Shorten commit ID.
- Timestamp and author.
- Commit message.
- Optionally decorations of refs, containing:
  - `HEAD → <branch>` appears for the commit pointed by HEAD.
    Shows which branch HEAD is pointing to.
  - `HEAD` — as above but in detached HEAD.
  - Branches and lightweight/annotated tags decorating the commit.

3.2. `git commit` — creating a new commit (growing the graph)

Documentation: ***git commit*** [https://git-scm.com/docs/git-commit]

In this chapter we will be developing/expanding/growing the graph in the most common way, specifically:

- When HEAD points to some branch.
- Using `git commit` command.

It will show us how the work with the branches looks like.

One can see refs as a way of decorating the graph. A commit pointed by a ref can be seen as 'decorated' by this ref. A decoration being a branch can be moved from one commit to another. Moreover, during committing Git automatically moves the branch to the new commit — the just created one.

3.2.1. Commands used

Although it might be counterintuitive, you have to remember, that commits (their contents) are **not** created from some random points in time, but from the **explicitly indicated** (most often with `git add` command) contents of all individual files.

We will be using several commands:

git init

Creates a Git repository (`.git` subdirectory in the current directory).

git add

Adds specified files' contents to the project state, which is assumed to be saved in the next commit. The contents added is the current contents of the files. In particular, if a file is changed after `git add` command was executed, and you want the new content to be saved, you have to execute `git add` command again.

git commit

Saves the changes prepared by `git add`.
Creates a new commit.
The saved state of the project will consist of files with the following contents:

- Files from the previous state (files, on which the `git add` command was not used) — the previous, unchanged contents.
- Files added by **git add** command — the changed contents (for a given file the last `git add` wins).

git branch

Creates a new branch: `git branch <branch-name> [<commit>]`
`<commit>` defaults to HEAD.

git checkout

Switches to a branch/commit `git checkout <branch-name>`.

In general `git checkout` performs complicated actions, what will be described later. All you need to know now is that it switches HEAD to the given branch or commit (detached HEAD). You use this command when during developing one branch you want to switch to developing another one.

3.2.2. First attempts

For now, we are just playing with the graph and don't care about the content of the project. And there we come across a little technical problem.

Git introduces itself as *"stupid content tracker"*, but sometimes it tries to defend the user, so that they don't do silly things. One of these is creating a commit with the same content as its parent has. As you remember, the purpose of committing is to create the history of the project content. So, there is nothing reasonable to be saved if nothing has changed.

Failed experiment

```
mkdir experiment7
cd experiment7
git init
touch x.txt ①
git add x.txt ②
git commit -m"Add x.txt" ③
git alog
git commit -m"Nothing new in project" ④
git alog
echo x >> x.txt  ⑤
git commit -m"Nothing new to be committed" ⑥
git add x.txt ⑦
git commit -m"Implement sth. in x.txt" ⑧
git alog
```

① Creating empty file x.txt.

② Telling Git to save file x.txt in the next commit with the file's current (empty) content.

③ Creating the first commit.

④ Git isn't creating any commit!

⑤ Modifying x.txt file.

⑥ Git still isn't creating any commit, because it wasn't told to save the new content of x.txt!

⑦ Telling Git, that in the next commit, the new x.txt content is to be saved.

⑧ A new commit has been created.

This experiment failed because ④ hasn't created a new commit. This problem can be solved in several ways:

- Always modify project and add changes to the new commit. It was done above.
- Force Git to accept commits that brings nothing new. This is what the `stupid-*` commands do!

Later in this chapter we will be using the mix of the commands:

- normal — wherever possible,
- stupid-<sth> — to force Git to execute such stupid commands.

3.2.3. Some exercises

Developing branches, creating branches (to develop them later)

```
mkdir stupid
cd stupid
git init
git stupid-commit root
git stupid-commit a
git stupid-commit b
git branch foo ①
git stupid-commit f1 ②
git branch bar ③
```

① Branch foo will start here (at current HEAD).

② master is still the growing branch.

③ Branch bar will start here (at current HEAD).

Developing branch bar

```
git checkout bar ①
git stupid-commit x
git stupid-commit y
```

① Switching in order to develop branch bar, starting at the commit with the f1 commit message.

Developing branch foo

```
git checkout foo ①
git stupid-commit k
git stupid-commit l
git stupid-commit m
```

① Switching in order to develop branch bar, starting at the commit with the b commit message.

Now branch foo grew independently of branch bar.

Developing branch master

```
git checkout master
git stupid-commit o
```

```
git stupid-commit p
```

git alog shows, that we have three branches growing from one common commit (the one with the b commit message). Additionally, master and bar have another common commit (the one with the f1 commit message), from which they diverge.

```
* c952503 2023-06-17 16:45 Jacek Drag p (HEAD -> master)
* 7b2687e 2023-06-17 16:45 Jacek Drag o
| * 03b0464 2023-06-17 16:44 Jacek Drag m (foo)
| * 464e17a 2023-06-17 16:44 Jacek Drag l
| * d0576cd 2023-06-17 16:44 Jacek Drag k
| | * b99b950 2023-06-17 16:44 Jacek Drag y (bar)
| | * 52e6d5c 2023-06-17 16:44 Jacek Drag x
| |/
|/|
* | 01ab47f 2023-06-17 16:44 Jacek Drag f1
|/
* c09105f 2023-06-17 16:43 Jacek Drag b
* bdeb9f5 2023-06-17 16:43 Jacek Drag a
* 1858e15 2023-06-17 16:43 Jacek Drag root
```

Basic commands:

- Creating a branch starting from a given commit:

```
git branch <new-branch> [<commit>]
```

<commit> defaults to HEAD.

- Switching to another branch/commit (in order to develop it):

```
git checkout <branch-or-commit>
```

- Creating a branch starting from a commit and switching to the branch in order to develop it. So, two commands from above in one:

```
git checkout -b <new-branch> [<commit>]
```

<commit> defaults to HEAD.

3.3. `git merge` — joining the branches

Documentation: *git merge* [https://git-scm.com/docs/git-merge]

As we already know how the branches can grow, let's take a look at how they can merge.

Intention is:
Changes in the project can be made for different reasons and by different people at the same time. It will often make several branches grow independently, or one branch grow in several different directions. But the repository is one, intended to track all the changes. To do that, you have to reconcile all independently grown branches.
You do this in two ways:

- *merge*
- *rebase*, meaning reapplying commits from the merged branch

Nomenclature is a little bit complicated, because although merge and rebase can be seen as two different (with the similar purpose, which is reconciling discrepancies) operations, rebase can be as well seen as an option of the merge command `git merge --rebase`.

In this chapter we will describe merge only. Rebase will be described in *Rebasing — transplanting branches*.

We will also ignore the possible issues with merging contents of the individual files. Our goal is still only (and as much!) getting along with the commit graph. Later, in the *Merge conflicts*, we will consider reconciling changes of the individual files in details, putting emphasis on the reconciliation of conflicted changes of the same file, which is called *conflicts resolving*. Let's just mention here that Git may try to merge the contents of the file which has changed in two branches.

Merging is creating a new commit, which has the merged branches (appropriate commits — tips of the branches being merged) on its parents list. It happens sometimes that the new commit isn't created. It is a very important case of merging two branches. It's called *fast-forward merge*, and it will be described separately. Commit that has several parents is called a *merge commit*.

To merge, `git merge` command is used:

- One switches to the main branch — `git checkout <main>`.
- Then one merges the branch being merged **to** the main branch — `git merge <to-be-merged>`.

There are two kinds of merge:

three-way merge

It's just the most common merge. Two branches are included in it — main and the one you want to merge (which changes you want to incorporate into the main branch).

The 'three-way merge' term will be explained in a while.

Right now let's notice the following features of the three-way merge:

- Parents list is **two-element** — some branch is merged to the main branch.
  This is the list, so the order matters. First commit comes from the main branch, and the second comes from the merged branch.
  In a very special case, that is fast-forward merge, parents list is one-element. In this case no new commit is created, but the branch (the ref) is moved instead. It will be described more precisely later.
- Git merges contents of the individual files. For each problematic file (with conflicted changes) Git marks them in the result file. If any conflict has occurred, operation won't be finished. Git raises *merge conflict* error and the user has to deal with it; has to resolve the conflicts. Operation can be finished after the user resolves all the conflicts (file by file). It is also possible to step back — to abort the whole merge operation.

octopus merge

Most likely the reader will never come across octopus merge.

- Parents list is **more than two-element** — several branches are merged to the main branch.
- If a conflict arises, all files stay untouched. Git kind of automatically aborts the merge operation.

Preparing conflict in file `file.txt` *in branches* `foo`, `bar` *and* `master`

```
git stupid-reset-to-root
echo master > file.txt
git add file.txt
git commit -m"on master"
git checkout -b foo $(git rev-list --max-parents=0 HEAD)
echo foo > file.txt
git add file.txt
git commit -m"on foo"
git checkout -b bar $(git rev-list --max-parents=0 HEAD)
echo bar > file.txt
git add file.txt
git commit -m"on bar"
git checkout master
git alog
```

Merge attempt (three-way merge)

```
git merge foo
cat file.txt
```

```
git merge --abort
```

```
git merge foo bar
cat file.txt
```

As you can see, after three-way merge attempt file file.txt contains kind of connected changes from both branches foo and master. However, after the octopus merge attempt, file file.txt stays untouched. Although none of these file contents is something you want to end up with, in the first case you can clearly see conflicts that have to be resolved. In the second case the user is told that Git didn't try to help with the merge.

3.3.1. *Feature/topic branch*

A feature branch or a topic branch is an often used term. Technically, it is just a normal branch, and the feature/topic term just emphases that the branch was created to develop some specific feature in it. They should be as short-lived as possible so that they don't introduce too many problems with integration and merge conflicts.

3.3.2. **Regular merge**

As mentioned, merge commit parents list is a list indeed, not a set. It is important which branch is being merged to which. In other words: which branch is intended to be incorporated into which.

Let's switch to the main branch and merge the second one.

Merging feature to master (incorporating feature into master)

```
git checkout -b feature
git stupid-commit acommit
git checkout master
git stupid-merge feature
git slog
```

Graph after the merge

```
*   59adfe2 2023-06-28 19:58 Jacek Drag merging feature (HEAD -> master)
|\
| * 6a7cb0a 2023-06-28 19:58 Jacek Drag acommit (feature)
|/
```

```
* f7a842d 2023-05-03 14:36 Jacek Drag second commit
```

Notice how asterisks and dashes show the parent relationship. You can see, that:

- Commit with the acommit message occurs in two branches
  - feature
  - master

    because branch feature has been merged to master.
- HEAD points to the merge commit, i.e. the commit which has two commits on its parents list.

3.3.3. *Fast-forward merge*

Now let's consider situation, in which the main branch wasn't developed.

```
git stupid-reset-to-root
git branch feature
git checkout feature
git stupid-commit m
```

You want to merge branch feature. Does the situation differ from the previous one? What is going to happen? The chapter title and the questions above suggest that the situation is different indeed. Well, let's find out:

```
git checkout master
git merge feature
```

Git answered:

```
Updating a6691e3..95ccc4f
Fast-forward
```

Let's find out what commits are these and how the merge commit looks like.

```
git slog
```

There is no merge commit! Branches master and feature are pointing to the **same** commit.

Alright, let's try again:

```
git merge feature
```

The answer:

```
Already up to date.
```

History:

```
git slog
```

No changes! Why? Git has realized that the branch being merged doesn't have any alternative history in comparison to the main branch, they didn't grow in two different ways. feature is simple a (linear) continuation of master. In other words: feature is continuing growth of master, master is pointing to some place in the feature's history of growth. Thus, instead of creating unnecessary objects, it is enough to change the tip of master — move ref (which is master) along the changes line set by feature. After that feature is incorporated into master, and both branches point to the same commit.

Actually, Git may be forced to create merge commit even in this case.

```
git stupid-reset-to-root
git branch feature
git checkout feature
git stupid-commit m
git checkout master
git merge --no-ff -m"no ff forced" feature
git slog
```

For example, it can be done to keep the history of **when** and by whom the changes have been merged. However, a very useful and powerful feature gets lost: **immutability**. As you know, commits are immutable. Thus, if **after the merge** the new tip of the main branch is **the same** commit as the tip of the merged branch before merge, then **everything** valid for this commit **before** the merge stays valid after the merge. So it is valid for the main branch as well!
In particular, **after the merge**, one does not have to do again anything that was done **before**. Most likely — depending on the established process — it covers:

- Building artifacts (images etc.). **They are already built!**
- Running tests. **They have already passed!**

Moreover, if in the meantime the main branch has grown (perhaps some other branch was merged to it), then the merge will not be a fast-forward merge anymore. What assures that a fast-forward merge is always secure! Secure, meaning if the merge was indeed fast-forward, conclusions above are for sure correct. And if it turns out, that the merge is not fast-forward, then the branch being merged is **not** integrated with the main branch. Which means it has to be integrated (while working with fast-forward, most likely rebase will be better than merge), and after the integration is done, the conclusions will still be valid!

That is why I personally prefer working with fast-forward merge. At least for the two-pizzas teams. The open-source situation can be different.

This kind of work is more often called working with rebase, then with fast-forward (in opposite to work with regular merge), because rebase is usually more visible — it is executed many times — but in fact it is all about finishing with fast-forward merge.

3.3.4. git merge-base — the base of three-way merge

Documentation: *git merge-base* [https://git-scm.com/docs/git-merge-base]

In the three-way merge one can easily spot candidates for two sides — those are the two branches. More precisely: tips of these branches (the commits pointed by these branches). Let's say, that they are commits A and B. The third side is so-called *merge base*, which is the first common ancestor of commits A and B. More precisely: starting from commits A and B and using the ancestor relationship, one traverses the graph (in the root direction) and searches for the first commit where these two paths first meet together.

git merge-base is the command for finding out the merge base.

One merge base for branches master *and* feature

```
git stupid-reset-to-root
git stupid-commit baza
git branch feature
git stupid-commit a
git stupid-commit b
git checkout feature
git stupid-commit x
git stupid-commit y
git stupid-commit z
git checkout master
git alog
git merge-base --all master feature ①
git stupid-merge feature
git alog
git show ②
```

① Branches have diverged and their merge base is the commit with message 'baza'.

② In the second line you can see the parents list — it is two-element. The commit from branch master is the first element of the list.

This example can be treated as a standard — two branches diverged (in the merge base), then they were developed independently. Ultimately, they have been merged.

Generally, branches can interweave in a more complicated way, and they can have several merge bases.

Two merge bases for branch-a *and* branch-b

```
git stupid-reset-to-root

git branch branch-a
git branch branch-ca

git checkout branch-a
git stupid-commit baza-1
git branch branch-cb
git stupid-commit a1

git checkout branch-ca
git stupid-commit baza-2
git branch branch-b
git stupid-commit c1

git checkout branch-cb
git stupid-commit cb

git checkout branch-b
git stupid-commit b1
git stupid-merge branch-cb

git checkout branch-a
git stupid-merge branch-ca

git branch -D branch-ca branch-cb

git alog
git merge-base --all branch-a branch-b
git stupid-merge branch-b
git show
```

3.3.5. Octopus merge

```
git stupid-reset-to-root
git branch o1
git branch o2
git stupid-commit 0
git checkout o1
git stupid-commit 1
git checkout o2
git stupid-commit 2
git checkout master
git stupid-octopus o1 o2 ①
git alog
git show ②
```

① Merging branches o1 and o2.

② In the second line you can see the parents list — it is three-element, and the first commit is from branch master.

3.3.6. Forcing merging behaviour

By default, git merge uses *fast-forward* wherever it can. However, this behaviour can be changed with the command's parameters:

--ff   Execute *ff* if possible, create the merge commit if not.
     This is the default.

--no-ff   Don't execute *ff*, even if it's possible. Always create the merge commit.

--ff-only Execute *ff* if possible, raise error if not.

--rebase Rebase (will be described later).

--squash This doesn't create a new commit but creates the ready to be committed state of the project, the state is the same as it would be after the merge.

3.4. Addressing expressions — traversing graph, sets of commits

Documentation: *gitrevisions* [https://git-scm.com/docs/gitrevisions]

As you know, commits are identified by the commit ID (SHA-1, hash). Along with ancestors relationship they create acyclic, directed graph. Thanks to the refs (like branches, annotated tags), some of the nodes of the graph (commits) can be easily reached.

But is it possible to reach any other commits in any other way than by refs or commits ID?

Well, it is. Git allows the user to identify commits by some *expressions*. By these expressions, you can reference:

- commits
- any Git objects (see *Git objects*) — trees, blobs, tags
- sets of commits

Most often expressions identifying commits are used, but the others can be useful as well. Commands used for calculating the expressions values are:

- *git rev-parse* [https://git-scm.com/docs/git-rev-parse]
- *git rev-list* [https://git-scm.com/docs/git-rev-list]

These are complicated in general. Here is the simplest form:

```
git rev-parse <expressions>
```

displays *revision*, that is SHA-1 of the object/objects specified by `<expressions>`.

 In many Git commands branches names etc. are passed as parameters. In reality, most often appropriate expressions can be used. A branch name is a special example of the simplest expression.

Some commands can get as parameters expressions that might not be obvious for the user, such as pushing a blob, instead of a commit.

3.4.1. Expressions identifying a commit

Most often used and the simplest expressions are:

- branch names, tags
- HEAD

Below **rev** will stand for some expression addressing a certain commit.

More complicated expressions that are most often used, are those using operators:

- tilde: ~
- roof: ^

rev~[n]

References the n-th ancestor of rev. For the merge commits it walks along the main inheritance line, i.e. it always picks the first parent from the list.

n defaults to 0, for n = 0 it just references rev.

Some identities

- rev~0 = rev
- rev~1 = rev~
- rev~~ = rev~2
- rev~~2 = rev~3
- rev~3~2 = rev~5

We are just summing the amount of tildes, and that is how we calculate the amount of generations for which we have to go backwards along the main inheritance line.

rev^[n]

References the n-th commit on the parents list of rev.

n defaults to 0, for n = 0 it just references rev.

Some identities

- rev^0 = rev
- rev^1 = rev^
- rev^1^1 = rev^^
- rev^1^2 = rev^^2

There is no summing here. Every single roof in the expressions above references another parents list.

Let's notice that — so to speak accidentally — we have:

- rev~0 = rev^0 = rev
- rev~ = rev^ = rev~1 = rev^1
- rev~~ = rev^^
- rev~~~ = rev^^^
- etc.

However, if tilde is followed by a number (different from 0 and 1), let's say n, the rev~n expression means something totally different from rev^n.

One could say that tilde is going backwards vertically, always choosing the most right direction (in the graph drown by git log --graph). On the other hand, roof goes horizontally along the parents list.

Tilde appears to be easier in usage (it's easier to type rev~5 than rev^^^^^). But roof must be used in order to turn from the main inheritance path.

Small experiment

```
git rev-parse HEAD HEAD~0 HEAD^0 HEAD~ HEAD^
git rev-parse master master~0 master^0 master~ master^
```

<refname>@{<n>}

These expressions (with <n> positive) are calculated based on *reflog* (see **Reflog**). <refname> can be skipped. In that case, the current branch will be used. Most often <refname> is a branch name but, among others, HEAD can be used as well.

@{-<n>}

    The negative values reference previous HEAD values (branches/commits).

```
git checkout @{-1}
git checkout -
```

[<branchname>]@{upstream}

    References the *upstream* of <branchname>, provided it is set.

    <branchname> can be skipped, then the current branch will be used.

    @{upstream} can be abbreviated to @{u}, so @{u} is the shortest form referencing the upstream of the current branch.

@

    @ alone is an abbreviation for HEAD.

3.4.2. Expressions identifying other Git objects

The previous expressions reference commits. Other expressions can be used to reference other Git objects.

```
rev^{<type>}
```

where *type* is optional and defaults to commit. Other possibilities are tree, blob and tag.

Let's say, that there is tag *v1.1* in the repository. In that case, expression v1.1 references this tag itself, and the v1.1^{} (that is v1.1^{commit}) expression references the commit decorated by the tag.

```
git show --name-only
git rev-parse master^{tree}
```

3.4.3. Versions of blobs and trees

<rev>:<path> — values stored in commits

    This references the value (blob/tree) of file/directory <path> stored in <rev>.

    For instance, HEAD~:README is content of file README stored in the 'previous' commit. master:README is content of that file stored in (the tip of) branch master.

    How can you reference to the project main directory (that is how to calculate HEAD^{tree}) in that notation? It will be HEAD: (with empty <path>).

:[<n>:]<path> — values stored in the index

> This references the file content (blob) of <path> stored in the index as version <n> (see *Merging in the index*).
>
> <n> defaults to 0. It is the current file content. Others possible values are 1, 2 and 3. They are used to mark merge conflicts.
>
> Thus, git rev-parse :README.md references the current (not conflicted) *README.md* file content stored in the index.

Having the file/tree value, you can display its content using git cat-file command, e.g.

```
git cat-file -p HEAD:README.md ①
git cat-file -p HEAD~: ②
```

① *README.md* file content from the current commit.

② Project main directory value from the previous commit.

3.4.4. Expressions referencing commits ranges

Some commands don't operate on single commits, but on commit sets (ranges).

<rev>

> In that context <rev> expression means reflexive-transitive complement of the parent relationship. Meaning all commits that are reachable from <rev>, i.e. the ones reachable by the ancestor relationship. Let's remember that a commit is considered to be reachable from itself.

^<rev>

> References commits unreachable from <rev>.

<rev1>..<rev2> — two dots, 'missing commits'

> One could say, that this expression references 'missing commits'. I.e. commits reachable from the <rev2>, but unreachable from the <rev1>. In other words, these from the commit <rev2> history, which are missing in the commit <rev1> history.
>
> This is an abbreviation for the ^<rev1> <rev2>. That range is used, among others, during the git rebase operation.

<rev1>...<rev2> — three dots, symmetric difference

> I.e. commits reachable from <rev1> or <rev2>, but not from both.

In both cases (two and three dots) you can skip <rev1> as well as <rev2>. They default to HEAD.

[<range>, ...]

> Some of the expressions above you can put one after another, which means the common part of the individual ranges.

E.g. `git log rev1 rev2 ⋯`.

4. History rewriting

4.1. Introduction

4.1.1. Review

- Commit is immutable.
- Especially the parents list of a commit cannot change.
- As a result, once created, any part of graph **cannot** change.
- But the graph can grow!
  You can add new commits to the existing graph (freely shaping the parents list of the added commit!).

4.1.2. Parent relationship and child relationship

It can be said that the parents list of a commit establishes a binary relationship on the set of commits. Let's call it *parent relationship*: a commit has a parent.

Reversing the parent relationship, we get *child relationship*: a commit has a child. This is more 'dynamic' view of the graph.

Let's consider two commits: CHILD and PARENT.

From the parent relationship:

- CHILD **has a parent**: any commit from the parents list of commit CHILD,

we get the child relationship:

- PARENT **has a child**: any commit having commit PARENT on its parents list.

Notice the differences — with the accuracy to the optional garbage collection of the unreachable commits (see **Garbage collection**), we have:

- Parent relationship is 'static', set once and for all.
  The commit parents list **never** changes.
- Child relationship is 'dynamic', it is never definitely set.
  The children set of a given commit can **always** be extended.

As a result:

- Starting from a commit, let's say LEAF, its ancestors (parents, grandparents etc.) graph is **always** the same, no matter how many commits you add!

- Starting from a commit, let's say ROOT, its descendants (children, grandchildren, etc.) list can **always** be extended!

4.1.3. Commit history

Let's introduce some definitions:

***The full history of commit A* in a given repository**
> is a subgraph of this repository, specified by commit **A** and the ancestor relationship.

***A history of commit A* in a given repository**
> is any coherent subgraph of the full history of commit **A**, containing commit **A**.
> In that case coherent means that each of its commits can be reached from commit **A** by ancestor relationship.

Again:
The definition becomes more dynamic and intuitive after reversing the relationship: from ancestor to descendant.
Then, *the full history of commit A* is a history of commits from the root to commit **A**.
And *the history of commit A* is a history of commits from some commit (or group of commit) to commit **A**.

One could say, that this perspective is more 'dynamic'. That new commits **are created** what **shapes** new history. In opposite, from the 'static' perspective, the history **is described** by the immutable relationship.

4.1.4. Immutable but rewritable

Now we know what the history of a commit is. Let's start to *rewrite* it.

Analogy to the historians work is accurate:

- The history cannot be changed.
  It was as it was, and it will always stay the way it was. Although, it can be hard to discover, to get known.
- But the history **can be rewritten**.
  During rewriting, it can be changed, or even counterfeit.

It turns out that Git not only perfectly manages creating the graph, that is documenting the real history, but also can be vey helpful during its rewriting. It may not be clear what might be the purpose of rewriting the history but in fact, it opens lots of possibilities!

In this part of the book we are still just playing with the graph, and we skip the problem of conflicts. Conflicts will be investigated later.

4.2. `git reflog` — the local history of refs changes

Documentation: *git reflog* [https://git-scm.com/docs/git-reflog]

First, you will learn how to review the changes made.

Git stores the changes history of individual refs in a structure called *reference logs*, abbreviated: *reflog*. Notice, that we are talking about the changes of a ref (most often branch), not about history of a commit from the previous chapter.

Reconstruction of those changes can be vey helpful. For example, you can restore the branch after accidentally deleting it.

Notice that reflog is **not** the element of the Git database. It is **not** being transmitted between the repositories also. It's just an additional structure, used to store the *local* work history.

To see, how reflog is stored you can run:

```
tree .git/logs
```

With command:

```
git reflog [show] [<ref>]
```

you can investigate how the value of <ref> has been changing.

- <ref> defaults to HEAD, but you can use a branch name.
- show is the default subcommand of git reflog. There are some other subcommands, but they will not be described in this guide.

This command is actually an abbreviation of the command:

```
git log -g --abbrev-commit --pretty=oneline [<ref>]
```

A small experiment

```
git stupid-commit aaa
git stupid-commit bbb
git stupid-commit ccc
```

reference log — HEAD

```
git reflog -3
```

Result

```
fa89e2a (HEAD -> master) HEAD@{0}: commit: ccc
b996353 HEAD@{1}: commit: bbb
87c6b25 HEAD@{2}: commit: aaa
```

Reference log — master

```
git reflog -3 master
```

Result

```
fa89e2a (HEAD -> master) master@{0}: commit: ccc
b996353 master@{1}: commit: bbb
87c6b25 master@{2}: commit: aaa
```

Normal log

```
git slog -3
```

Result

```
* fa89e2a 2021-12-31 13:25 Jacek Drag ccc (HEAD -> master)
* b996353 2021-12-31 13:25 Jacek Drag bbb
* 87c6b25 2021-12-31 13:25 Jacek Drag aaa
```

Reflog's rows show:

- Command that changed the ref.
- Commit pointed by ref after the change was made.
- The way of referencing the commit: <ref>@{n}. n says how many steps it goes back. These expressions change after each change of the ref. After the next change one have to go back one step further.

You can see, that git commit with bbb commit message created commit b996353 (which became new tip of branch master).

If the list displayed by git reflog is too long you can use -<n>, e.g.

```
git reflog -10
```

 git reflog [-<n>] [<ref>] allows to see last n local changes of ref <ref> (HEAD by default).

4.3. git commit --amend — amendment of the last commit

Let's say you have created some commit, but you have made a mistake in the commit message. Now you want to correct it.

The command used to do this is: git commit --amend. The simplest of the history rewriting commands.

Wrong comment

```
git stupid-commit aax
git alog
```

Comment amendment

```
git stupid-amend aaa
git alog
```

Now HEAD is pointing to the corrected commit (the one having message aaa). But what has happened to aax, why isn't it visible in the log? It was the tip of the branch, so it was indirectly pointed by HEAD. Let's search for it in the reflog.

```
git reflog -5
```

or

```
git reflog -5 master
```

There it is!

```
3513fae (HEAD -> master) HEAD@{0}: commit (amend): aaa
```

```
aff58b9 HEAD@{1}: commit: aax
```

The commit with message aax is not being pointed by any ref at the moment. As a result, it is considered unreachable. But it is still stored in the repository. And it isn't totally unreachable! If you **know** its commit ID (or a prefix of it), you can reach it by giving the commit ID directly. That is what you have done — you have found the commit ID (aff58b9) in the reflog.

Ok, having the commit ID of the old commit, let's display a graph containing that old commit, too.

You can do it this way: git slog displays HEAD history. But you can give it other commits, history of which you also want to see.

```
git slog <commit 1> <commit 2> ...
```

Moreover, you can use addressing expressions there (see *Addressing expressions*).

Let's try:

```
git slog HEAD HEAD@{1}
```

or

```
git slog master master@{1}
```

Nice! You can see the old commit (unreachable from any ref). You can also see that his parent did not change. However, master and HEAD switched to commit aaa.

You could see, that author and time are also the same. Let's prove it:

```
git show master
git show master@{1}
```

Let's try again, but without changing anything!

```
git commit --amend --allow-empty --no-edit
```

```
git slog master master@{1} master@{2}
```

Commit bbb has three children now: aax, aaa and new aaa.

The previous commit message version was better. But you want the branch to point to the commit with aax. Of course, you could do the next `git commit --amend`. But a new commit would be created then! You will learn how to use `git reset` command soon. But even with the current knowledge, you could restore the branch to the reflog value. After all, refs are just decorations of commits!

Example: setting commit in the branch.

Version with a temporary branch

```
git checkout -b tmp ①
git branch master -f <commit-ID> ②
git alog ③
git checkout master ④
git branch -D tmp ⑤
git alog
```

① Necessary to execute the next command. The problem is that `git branch -f` cannot operate on the current branch.

② The actual resetting of the branch (that is the ref), so that it points to the given `<commit-ID>`.

③ Checking, that the branch is pointing to the `<commit-ID>`.

④ Returning to `master`.

⑤ Deleting the temporary branch.

Detached HEAD version

```
git checkout HEAD^{commit} ①
git branch master -f <commit-ID>
git checkout master
```

① Switching to the current commit in detached HEAD state. It could be `git checkout <commit-ID>` as well.

Version with temporarily deleting the branch

```
git checkout <commit-ID>
git branch -D master
git checkout -b master ①
```

① Creating branch `master` (pointing to the current commit).

With commit `--amend` not only the commit message can be changed but also the commit content.

```
touch xx
git add xx
git stupid-amend "Add xx"
git slog
git show --name-only
```

 git commit `--amend` abandons the latest commit. Then, using its parents list, author and index, creates a new commit. It allows to 'change' the commit message and the saved project state.

4.4. git revert — undoing changes previously made

Documentation: *git revert* [https://git-scm.com/docs/git-revert]

git revert command, similarly to git cherry-pick, operates on existing commits. But instead of reapplying the changes made by the original commit, it creates a commit undoing the changes.

Let's say you have done some changes two commits backwards. But the changes were pretty poor, and now you want to cancel them. git commit `--amend` won't help as it operates on the last commit. If the poor commit is <commit-ID>, you can execute:

```
git revert <commit-ID>
```

Now, a new commit undoing the changes is created. So you have two commits in the history, now. One introducing the changes and the second one reverting them.

In some situations, you may want to delete those commits from the history permanently. It can be done. git rebase and git reset commands could help.

4.5. git cherry-pick — transplanting commit/set of commits

Documentation: *git cherry-pick* [https://git-scm.com/docs/git-cherry-pick]

Here is another situation in which the history rewriting is very helpful:
Let's say Bob is developing branch master, and Alice is developing branch feature. Alice has corrected some mistakes and committed the fixes. Bob needs these fixes in his branch, so he asks Alice to implement her changes to branch master as well. She answers: The fix is done in commit 11abcd. If you want, just copy this commit to your branch.

The idea is: Alice's fix **has changed** the project (its content) in some particular way. Bob would like to make the **same** change in his project's content. git commit `--amend` will not help. Similarly, switching Bob's branch to Alice's commit would change the whole project content and this is not what Bob wants. Bob only has the last and the current commit from branch feature at his disposal.

The command which does the job is git cherry-pick.

Small experiment

```
git stupid-reset-to-root
git checkout -b feature
git stupid-commit a
git stupid-commit b
git checkout master
sleep 1
git alog
git stupid-cherry-pick feature
git alog
```

Verification

```
git show master
git show feature
```

You can see that:

- As with --amend the author and the creation time data have been copied.
- The commit message has also been copied.
- The parent has changed.
- It is important, that the new commit changes its parent the same way the original commit changes its parent. It cannot be seen here because stupid commits are empty, but this is exactly what cherry-pick does.
- The original commit is still reachable. It's still pointed by branch feature.

 git cherry-pick <commit> calculates the *patch* that transforms the content of <commit>'s parent into the content of <commit> itself. Then the patch is applied to the content of current commit, creating this way a new commit.

 cherry-pick usage causes the commit duplication. Therefore, it would be best not to use it, as duplication is always suspicious.

The command is more powerful — using expressions (see **Commit ranges**) you can copy several commits at once. The commits will be copied one by one.

4.6. `git rebase` — transplanting branches

Documentation: *__git rebase__* [https://git-scm.com/docs/git-rebase]

The situation is identical to *__git merge__*. There are two branches (having some commit as their common ancestor). Let's say these branches are `master` and `feature` — somebody has been developing `master`, and you have been developing `feature` — and you want to reconcile changes made in both branches, so that the further graph development could have them both in one branch. Let's say you want `master`, and most precisely new commits from `master`, to be incorporated into `feature`.

`git merge` can be seen as merging the branches, `git rebase` can be seen as transplanting one branch on the tip of the other. After that operation the transplanted (copied) branch (feature), grows from the tip of the branch onto which it has been transplanted (`master`). This way it includes this tip in its new history.

As the commits are immutable, the situation is similar to `git commit --amend`. I.e. the **copies** of the commits are created. More precisely:

- The original commits from `feature` stay untouched.
- Onto the tip of `master`, as 'the new base', the copies of the commits from `feature` are applied. The branch `feature` itself starts to point to the last applied commit copy.
- The old, abandoned `feature` value (its old tip) can be found in the reflog, of course.

In the case of merge, you have to decide what you want to merge with what (which commit will come first on the parents list). Similar to rebase, you have to decide, which branch you want to be transplanted onto which (commits from which branch will come first in the graph). It is not as simple as it might seem.

4.6.1. Including changes of `master` in `feature` (integrating changes)

You want your code to be **integrated** with the 'main branch', because changes in the feature lasted so long that `master` managed to change in the meantime.

merge   `feature` is the current branch. You merge `master` to `feature`.
               `git checkout feature; git merge master.`

rebase   `feature` is the current branch. You rebase `feature` onto `master`.
               `git checkout feature; git rebase master.`

In both cases branch `master` stays untouched, unaware of the changes. But `feature` gets 'integrated'. That means it is changing the current value of `master`, now.

4.6.2. Including `feature` changes in `master` (incorporating changes)

You want to **finally incorporate** your new code into the 'main branch'.

merge	master is the current branch. You merge feature to master.
	`git checkout master; git merge feature.`
rebase	You could think that:
	master is the current branch, and you transplant master onto feature.
	That is not the case. Of course, you could do that, but there is a better way:

```
git checkout feature; git rebase master ①
git checkout master; git merge feature ②
```

① You repeat the previous step:

feature is the current branch. You transplant feature onto master.

Because you want — as the preliminary condition of including new code into master — this new code to **be integrated** with the master in advance.

② You switch to master and **merge** feature to master. It is a fast-forward merge! No new commit is created. master is just moved a little bit forward (to the transplanted feature).

Let's compare the graphs:

- In the case of merge, you will have a fusion of branches. The merge commit will be the fusion point of the branches.

The more often you integrate, the more complicated the graph will be.

- In the case of rebase, you will get a bamboo, each commit will have one parent only.

The resulting history will be linear, independently of the integrations' frequency. During work the diverges will be created, but they will be deleted during each 'integration' rebase. Even when developing a branch for a long time, you can have it integrated with the master all the time. It is your problem, if during development the incompatible changes will be created. You have to reconcile your code with the new changes in master on every rebase.

One more effect of using rebase and fast-forward:

If merge to master is fast-forward, there is no need to repeat anything that was executed on feature. The commit is **the same**, merged code is already integrated!

Whereas after the normal merge, one can never be sure if it was good before merge, it will also be good after. After merge the code can even stop compiling (some changes incompatible with feature made in master)!

Above, you can see that the usage of ff is more important than rebase. The property "merged code is always integrated and merge feature to master is always ff" can be achieved by merging master to feature before each feature to master merge. However, it is not done this way very often.

Merge and rebase are generally two competing ways of developing the graph. Most optimal for a given repository will be choosing only one of these ways.

4.6.3. The form of the command

The most complete form of merge command considered in this book is:

```
git rebase [-i] --onto <new-base> <upstream> <branch>
```

All parameters are optional.

```
git rebase [-i | --interactive] [--onto <new-base>] [<upstream> [<branch>]]
```

This command means: take the (missing) commits from <branch> from the place, in which it diverged with <upstream>. Transplant them onto <new-base>.

4.6.4. How it works

git rebase executing stages are:

- Calculating the list of commits to be transplanted.
- For the individual commits, calculating patches to be applied later. Each patch transforms the content of the commit's parent into the content of the commit itself.
- Switching to branch <branch> (if <branch> specifies a branch, a commit can be given as well).
- Changing HEAD to <new-base>.
- Application of the earlier calculated patches (kind of cherry-pick series).
  Application can be interactive (-i | --interactive), which allows to skip, join, or even split some commits into several new ones. This will be described in **Interactive rebase**.
- Moving branch <branch> to the latest commit and moving HEAD to <branch>.

The list of commits to be transplanted consists of the commits belonging to the history (see **Commit history**) of commit <branch>, not belonging to the history of commit <upstream>. That is, the transplanted set of commits is the range <upstream>..<branch> (see **Commit ranges**).

During patches application conflicts can occur, but we skip this problem for now.

4.6.5. Parameters and their default values

We will start from the general version of the command, and we will be considering individual parameters — their names and their purposes.

Let's consider two real life cases:

Using a feature branch

At certain moment you have diverged from some branch — let's say from `main` — creating new branch `feature`. Now you want to integrate `feature` with `main`, which has been also developed in the meantime. That means you want to transplant all new commits from `feature` onto the new tip of `main`.

So the command:

```
git rebase --onto <new-base> <upstream> <branch>
```

becomes:

```
git rebase --onto main main feature
```

Development of the same branch by many people
New branch hasn't been created. You are developing branch `master`, and your colleagues are developing it as well. Their changes are somehow applied to your repository (you will learn how in the second part of the book) as a branch named *origin/master*. From time to time, you want to integrate these two paths of the development. You do this by transplanting your changes onto *origin/master*.
In this case the command looks like this:

```
git rebase --onto origin/master origin/master master
```

<new-base>

The name `<new-base>` is self explaining — it is the 'new base'. That is a commit, onto which commits are transplanted.

<new-base> defaults to <upstream> (to the second parameter)
It makes sense, as indeed most often you want to transplant one branch onto the other one — `<branch>` onto `<upstream>`. In this case, `<upstream>` has two roles:

- The branch for which the list of missing commits is calculated (the commits created in `<branch>` and lacking in `<upstream>`).
- 'New base', i.e. the commit onto which the missing commits are to be transplanted.

So instead of:

```
git rebase --onto main main feature
```

enough is:

```
git rebase main feature
```

Instead of:

```
git rebase --onto origin/master origin/master master
```

enough is:

```
git rebase origin/master master
```

In general, you can transplant the commits onto any other commit if you only want to.

<branch>

<branch> name is adequate. Most often you **indeed** want to transplant a branch. At the end, your branch will be moved to the last transplanted commit.

<branch> defaults to HEAD.

During executing git rebase, HEAD most often points to the branch that is to be transplanted.

So instead of:

```
git rebase main feature
```

enough is:

```
git rebase main
```

Instead of:

```
git rebase origin/master master
```

enough is:

```
git rebase origin/master
```

In general, you can transplant commits from any commit history, missing in <upstream> history.

If you only want to.

<upstream>

<upstream> parameter name comes from its default value:
<upstream> defaults to HEAD@{upstream}.

Upstreams will appear in the second part of the book (see **Upstream**).

If the current branch has not set up its upstream, you cannot abbreviate:

```
git rebase main
```

to:

```
git rebase
```

Because Git doesn't know which missing commits you mean and where to transplant the commits:

```
Please specify which branch you want to rebase against.
See git-rebase(1) for details.

    git rebase '<branch>'
```

<branch> (acting here as <upstream> from the general command call) would default to the *upstream* of the current branch.

If *origin/master* **is** the *upstream* of master:

```
git rebase origin/master
```

can be abbreviated:

```
git rebase
```

Just to mention — if merge policy is set up to *rebase* for the current branch:

```
git pull
```

translates to:

```
git fetch
git rebase
```

In case when `master` is the current branch and `origin/master` is its upstream it translates to:

```
git fetch
git rebase --onto origin/master origin/master master
```

4.6.6. Interactive rebase

As mentioned, all the rebase commands above can be executed in the interactive mode. However, most often `<new-base>` and `<branch>` parameters are not used then. It is rather done this way:

```
git rebase -i <after-this-commit>
```

where `<after-this-commit>` is not a branch name, but a commit from HEAD history. Let's try to decode the command below:

- `<after-this-commit>` is the only given parameter, so it is both the `<upstream>` and `<new-base>` value.
- `<branch>` defaults to HEAD.

So the extended command looks like this:

```
git rebase -i --onto <after-this-commit> <after-this-commit> HEAD
```

Therefore, the list of the commits to be transplanted are 'missing commits'. That is those, which were created after `<after-this-commit>` up to HEAD (inclusive).

Now, what does 'interactive' mean? The patches list isn't instantly applied. Instead, the editor displaying this list is launched. The list can be edited then. The edited list is the one that will be applied after the editor will have been closed. In particular, if you don't change anything on the list, the operation result will be the same, as if it would be without `--interactive` option.

Sample list created by `rebase --interactive`

```
pick 2c8f0ac bbb ①
pick a211a8b ccc
```

```
  pick 5865432 aaa

  - Rebase 004cd13..5865432 onto 004cd13 (3 commands) ②
  -
  - Commands: ③
  - p, pick <commit> = use commit
  - r, reword <commit> = use commit, but edit the commit message
  - e, edit <commit> = use commit, but stop for amending
  - s, squash <commit> = use commit, but meld into previous commit
  - f, fixup <commit> = like "squash", but discard this commit's log message
  - x, exec <command> = run command (the rest of the line) using shell
  - b, break = stop here (continue rebase later with 'git rebase --continue')
  - d, drop <commit> = remove commit
  - l, label <label> = label current HEAD with a name
  - t, reset <label> = reset HEAD to a label
  - m, merge [-C <commit> | -c <commit>] <label> [# <oneline>]
  - .        create a merge commit using the original merge commit's
  - .        message (or the oneline, if no original merge commit was
  - .        specified). Use -c <commit> to reword the commit message.
  - ④
  - These lines can be re-ordered; they are executed from top to bottom.
  -
  - If you remove a line here THAT COMMIT WILL BE LOST.
  -
  - However, if you remove everything, the rebase will be aborted.
  -
```

① The calculated commits list. Here it has three elements.

② The information, on what basis this list was calculated (see the description of the parameters above and **Commit ranges**).

③ The list of commands that can be applied to each individual commit.

④ The information how to use the interactive mode.

Only two first columns matters on the commits list :

command   This can be abbreviated. Available commands with their abbreviations are listed on the command list. Some of them will be shortly described.

commit ID   Prefix is sufficient of course.

Column with the commit message is auxiliary. It helps to make decisions about individual rows.

In fact, the whole commits list is only a proposition. The list can be shaped in any way e.g. by adding any commit, even from outside the list.

Comments about some commands:

pick   Reapply the commit (the patch). This is inserted by default.

drop	Don't apply it. It is often easier to just delete the row.
squash/fixup	The two differ by the result's commit message only.
break	Allows to 'crush' the commit. Usage of *git reset* command is required to do this.

There are several possibilities to resign from rebase execution:

- Using *Reflog* after executing rebase and restoring the branch with *git reset* command.
- According to the tip put by Git in the file: delete all rows from the list.
- Close the editor in such way, that it returns with file saving error code. Git will not know what the user wanted to be done. Therefore, it will do nothing, just to avoid destroying something.
  With the vi editor this means typing :cq (in vi's insert mode).

At the end, interactive git rebase is an awesome way to reorganize the history.

git rebase -i <after-this-commit> proposes a list of commits created after <after-this-commit> to be applied (onto <after-this-commit>) again. Edition of the proposed commits list means deciding: which of them should actually be applied, which should be skipped, which should be squashed etc.

4.7. git reset doesn't create commits

Another important 'history rewriting' command is git reset but it will be described later (see *git reset*). At the moment, we are still concentrating on the commit graph only. From that perspective, even though git rebase is using reset, still as a final result you can see just the expanded graph. You don't have to know that there was some reset involved. The reset itself, although very useful for history rewriting, does not make the graph expand. It doesn't create new commits. In addition, *working dir* and *staging area* are needed to describe it (see *Working tree* and *Staging ara*).

4.8. git gc — garbage collection

Documentation: *git gc* [https://git-scm.com/docs/git-gc]

git gc executes lots of organizing and repository optimizing operations. From this book's perspective deleting unreachable commits is the most important.

That is, if some commit is unreachable from any ref, it will be removed from the repository at some point in time. It will be done automatically, because git gc is automatically launched by lots of others commands.

The kinds of refs keeping commits in the repository

- branches (all kinds)
- lightweight tags and annotated tags
- reflog elements
- index elements (see *Staging ara*)

Garbage collection has a lot of configuration options but usually there is no need to change anything. Default operations are good enough. By default, reflog elements are deleted after 90 days, and you hardly ever have to change this setting.

For example, one could expect that after rebasing old commits will be collected after about 3 months. I.e. after the old tip of the branch will be deleted from the reflog.

Normally there is no need to launch git gc manually.

 Commits that are unreachable from any ref will be deleted from the repository after some time.

5. Real work

5.1. Graphical tools — Git isn't a hardliner

This book focuses on working with command line. However, sometimes it is more efficient to use graphical tools, including IDE. This is especially true for comparing files contents and conflicts resolving.

It turns out that Git is not a hardliner. Even during work with command line, it allows to use graphical tools for some purposes! Specifically, difftool and mergetool can be configured. Personally, I usually use mergetool for conflicts resolving:

```
git mergetool
```

Example of mergetool configuration

```
git config --global merge.tool intellij-idea ①
git config --global mergetool.intellij-idea.cmd 'intellij-idea-ultimate merge $LOCAL $REMOTE
$BASE $MERGED' ②
```

① Defining a tool used for conflict resolving.

② Configuration of this tool (how to run it).

IDE can be also very useful for commit preparing. Especially creating a commit from only some selected changes can be much easier with IDE.

Normally, after creating a new file in the working tree, IDE asks if it should instantly add the file to the index. It is a good idea. Similarly, when deleting a file, it is better to instantly delete the file from the index.

5.2. Working tree/directory

Working tree is just the project directory (of course with all its files and subdirectories recursively). Often *working directory* term is used, but it is less precise. When someone says *working directory* it might be not clear if they mean *working tree* or just the directory that is the current one at the moment. So in the second case it could be some subdirectory of the working tree. By saying *working tree* always the whole project directory is meant.

One important thing: *.git* subdirectory is excluded, so *working tree* is the project directory without the repository.
You are working here: modifying files, compiling them, running tests etc. And eventually you want to save the changes. But, kindly reminder: Git does not save the changes, but the whole snapshots of the working tree.

It might seem to be simple, that creating a new commit is one command task: 'Save the current working tree state as the new commit'.

But it's much more complicated than that. It is not obvious whether you want to commit (save in the next commit) all files from the working tree. And whether what you want to save, should be saved in the exact current state or only some selected changes should be taken into account.

There we meet the stupid content tracker again. Git doesn't know and does not care about what you want to have in your upcoming commit. You have to explicitly indicate to Git what exactly should be saved. Git allows the user to specify very flexibly what (from the working tree) is to be saved as the commit. Of course, many possibilities mean greater complexity. It may turn out, that preparing a new commit is a really hard work. But it is worth it. It is rewarded with the comfort of usage of what has been created.

There are several approaches that can be taken when shaping commits. The most important factor on what approach is suitable, should be the fact of how much you care to keep the individual commits decent. Generally: the bigger and the longer the project is, the better organized the commits should be. If you work alone, and you are going to finish the work in two days, and you are not going to go back to it, the temporary junk files etc. won't probably bother you. Maybe even the state of the project which fails to build is acceptable for some commits. From time to time you will want to commit the whole working tree and that's it. However, if you work in the team, you will probably expect the project to build even if your colleagues change something, won't you? In particular, if you wanted to achieve CI/CD, **each** commit should be deployable. That means it has to be very decent. As a consequence, saving the whole working tree in some random moments is not going to work.

This intermediate guide is meant to give the reader a better understanding how Git really works. It will be helpful during hard work when less obvious situations occur. This is why it is good to learn how Git tracks the files.

It's good to know how Git sees, from the perspective of the upcoming commit, the files from the working tree. Namely, each file can be in one of the following states:

untracked/edited → **staged** → **committed**

 In fact, Git sees this in a more subtle way. It tracks each individual file not only as a whole, but considers the changes done as divided into several *hunks*, and can treat the individual hunks separately. It has a special importance during conflict resolving, what will be discussed in **Merge conflicts**.

The most difficult of these states is **staged**. That is: ready to be committed. And this is what you are going to learn about in the next chapter.

5.3. Index (*staging area*)

At the very beginning, let's settle some issues:

 Are the index and the staging area indeed exactly the same thing? **Yes**, they are two names of the **same** thing.

The index is stored in the *.git/index* file.

This topic is often mistaken even by experienced Git users. So let's emphasize the **proper** abstractions again.

 The staging area (also called the index) is the project state that will be saved with the upcoming git commit command.

 git commit **does not save content of the working tree but content of the index!**

Therefore, preparing a commit is putting the project files in the proper states into the staging area.

One can see an analogy to working with ACID, read committed database. When you have an **open transaction** in the database, you are modifying its contents:

- Adding some rows.
- Modifying some others.
- Deleting some others.

You can do this in many steps, and each next step can modify the rows modified in the previous steps. You can even:

- Modify rows that you have added earlier.
- Delete rows that you have added earlier.
- Restore rows that you have deleted earlier (might be hard).
- Roll back **all** the changes.

And all these changes (new state of the rows that are involved in the transaction) are invisible for the others until the changes are committed. During the commit the new database state is being saved and becomes visible for the other transactions.

The index can be seen as a modified project state:

- not committed yet
- not visible for the bystanders yet
- still modifiable,

which during committing will be (as a whole) saved and exposed as a new commit.

 The index also stores the information about merge conflicts, but it will be discussed later.

There is one more **very important** difference:

- In the database transaction, **only** the rows modified by this transaction are involved. In the meantime other transactions can change other (not modified by your transaction) rows (read-committed transaction). As a result, the state after commit doesn't have to be exactly the one from before the transaction with the changes applied.
- Staging area is the **whole** project content (serializable transaction).

After committing the created commit will contain the **exact** index content. While committing Git does not care about:

- what is in the working tree,
- what is in other commits,
- it makes no comparisons,
- it does not apply any patches,
- it takes the index content **as it is**. And **this exact** content is saved in the new commit.

One of the most common mistakes is thinking that it is the information about changes between the commit and its parent what is stored in the index.

I do want to convince you how it really works. Therefore, let's do some experiment with the *git ls-files* [https://git-scm.com/docs/git-ls-files] command. The command displays information about the files in the index and in the working tree.

Experiment

- Clone some small repository (so that there are no changes in the working tree).
- Execute the following commands and watch.

```
git status ①
git ls-files --stage ②
rm .git/index ③
git status ④
git ls-files --stage ⑤
git reset --hard ⑥
git status
git ls-files --stage
> zzz
git ls-files --stage ⑦
git add zzz
git ls-files --stage ⑧
git commit -m"Add zzz"
git ls-files --stage ⑨
```

① "nothing to commit"

② Listing the files in the index.

③ Deleting the index. Normally, never do that!

④ "Changes to be committed" contains all project files!

⑤ Because the index is empty! All the files were previously in the index but were deleted from there.

⑥ Restoring everything (especially the index) to the state from HEAD.

⑦ The index hasn't changed.

⑧ There is a new file in the index.

⑨ The index hasn't changed.

You can guess the meaning of the majority of the results displayed by `git ls-files`. Except for the mysterious zeros. This will be discussed with merge conflicts (see *Merge conflicts*).

From the `git status` *documentation*

Displays paths that have differences between the index file and the current HEAD commit, (...). The first are what you would commit by running git commit; (...)

From the `git add` *documentation*

The "index" holds a snapshot of the content of the working tree, and it is this snapshot that is taken as the contents of the next commit.

5.4. Preparing a new commit — hard work

As you know, preparing a new commit technically means putting the files into the index. Files need be structured in the way you want them in the upcoming commit. What's more, the index should contain these and only these files.

Let's assume that the project consists of 10000 files in 400 directories. It would be very unpractical to have to care about all the files instead of only about those which are going to be changed. And of course you don't have to! This is because HEAD is the starting point.
Namely, after commit operation is done situation looks like this:

- **HEAD** points to the new commit.
  Most often indirectly, as this is the current branch (its tip) which was moved to the new commit, and HEAD keeps pointing to that branch.
- **The index** contains exactly the same content as the new commit.
  The commit was created based on the index, and committing does not change the index! In other words: the index content is the same as the new commit content.

Using the modifying database analogy, you could say, that you have a new, empty transaction. The database state as a whole is exactly the same as after committing. So you can start making new changes.

The normal work is to:

- Modify/add/delete files in the working tree.
- Save some of the changed files in the index.
- Save the index as a new commit.

git add, git rm and other commands putting changes into the index are often executed many times before committing. You can examine the files added and the files eligible to be added with git status and git diff commands.

You can resign from part of/all changes written to the index. Luckily, rolling back the changes from the index doesn't have to cause rolling back them from the working tree.

5.4.1. Noticing changes made in the working tree in the index

In this chapter we will only consider adding changes to the index. That is the first arrow from: **untracked/edited** → **staged** → **committed**. Going against the tide (**untracked/edited** ← **staged**), that is resigning from the changes from the index is also possible. We will deal with it after learning the git checkout and git reset commands. With these commands you can even resign from the changes in a commit (**staged** ← **committed**).

git add — adding a new file content to the index

Documentation: *git add* [https://git-scm.com/docs/git-add]

To add the current content of a file from the working tree to the index you use the git add command. In the simplest case, it could be:

```
git add [--] [<pathspec>...]
```

Technically, Git finds the files compatible with <pathspec> in the working tree. And for each of these files, let's say <path>:

- Checks content of file <path> (the blob) in the working tree.
- Calculates hash of this blob.
- Adds the file content (the blob) to the map under the calculated hash.
- Saves to the index information that file <path> has content identified by the hash, now.

Of course, calculated hash can already exist in the database. There is no need to add it again in this case. You believe, that the old value mapped by the hash is exactly the same as the new one.

Possible forms of the <pathspec>

file   E.g. `git add dir/foo.txt`

directory   If a directory is given, all files from that directory will be added (recursively, from all its subdirectories).

***fileglob*, e.g. `*.c`**   All files will be added according to the pattern. You should pay attention to who is going to expand a pattern — Git or shell.

```
git add -n *.c    ①
git add -n \*.c   ②
```

① Expanded by shell — the files in the main directory only.

② Expanded by Git — the files in the whole directory structure.

The precise description of the <pathspec> can be found in the documentation (see ***pathspec*** [https://git-scm.com/docs/gitglossary#Documentation/gitglossary.txt-aiddefpathspecapathspec]).

Normally, the `git add` command requires passing some <pathspec>. These two options below allow not to pass any <pathspec>. In that case, the command operates on the whole working tree, independently of the subdirectory you are currently in (your current working directory!).

Option not requiring the <pathspec> being passed

(-A | --all)

Default option. In particular:

- Files absent in the index (present in the working tree) become added to the index.
- Files which disappeared from the working tree become deleted from the index.

(-u | --update)

> Narrowing down to files from the index (update of the files present in the index). In particular:
>
> - Files absent in the index (present in the working tree) are ignored.
> - Files which disappeared from the working tree become deleted from the index.

As -A is the default option, what's the difference between:

```
git add .
```

and

```
git add -A .
```

Well, there is no difference.

However, as mentioned above -A doesn't require passing any <pathspec>. And the difference between:

```
git add .
```

and

```
git add -A
```

depends on the directory in which the command is being executed. If in the main directory, there will be no difference. If in some subdirectory, git add . limits itself to this subdirectory, while git add -A works on the whole working tree.

Other sometimes useful options

   (-f | --force)   Forcing adding the ignored files (see *.gitignore*).

   (--chmod=(+|-)x)   The change (in the index only) of the file's execution permission.

Normally, git add operates on the whole files, but there are more advanced, less popular options as well. They allow to add the **selected changes** only and force nonstandard behaviour. Comparing two files contents, Git divides the changes into *hunks*. E.g. change of the first line is one hunk, and adding something at the end of the file is another hunk.

(-i | --interactive) [<subpath>]

Git itself checks which files differ from their equivalents in the index. Then Git asks about them individually if they should be added or to do something more subtle with them.

(-p | --patch) [<subpath>]

Interactive adding changes of the individual files hunks.

Let's say, that these are advanced options and as such they won't be described here in detail. The intermediate users can use the IDE tools to do such an advanced stuff.

Just notice that by adding some selected changes you can get the blob which is not the value of any file yet. To see the value you can use the command:

```
git cat-file -p :README.txt
```

Colon instructs the command to display the version of the file which is stored the index (see *Versions of blobs and trees*).

 git add command saves the current files states in the index. This includes deleting files that were deleted from the working tree.

If the file will be changed in the working tree again later, saving that change in the index requires subsequent git add execution.

git rm — deleting the file from the working tree and/or the index

Documentation: *git rm* [https://git-scm.com/docs/git-rm]

Command:

```
git rm [--] [<pathspec>...]
```

deletes files from the working tree and from the index.

- Similar to git add, <pathspec> can be in the *.c form.
- If any <path> is a directory name the -r option has to be used.

The file that is being deleted must not be changed in comparison to HEAD neither in the index nor in the working tree (but can be deleted from the working tree). Otherwise, it would cause the irreversible lost of the changed value (it doesn't exist in any commit).

If the file was deleted from the working tree only, it can be deleted from the index with git rm <file> or git add <file> command. But it (rm/add) can be done only once, that is as long as the file exists in the index. Later Git will complain, as it will be a file Git knows nothing about.

--cached	Deleting from index only, without any influence on the working tree. After committing the file will become untracked.
(-f | --force)	Skipping the check whether the file content is compatible with HEAD.
-r	Recursively deleting directories.

5.4.2. Undoing changes in the index

Undoing changes made in the working tree is easy, as it just means editing files on the disk. Undoing changes made to the index is harder. Maybe the most difficult thing is restoring a file deleted from the index. It can be done this way:

```
git checkout HEAD -- <file>
```

git checkout command will be described later. In the form above it reads the file content from the commit (HEAD in this example) and puts it into the working tree and into the index.

5.5. git commit — a piece of cake

Documentation: *git commit* [https://git-scm.com/docs/git-commit]

After preparing a new commit, you just have to commit the prepared project content, what creates a new commit object:

```
git commit
```

On that stage Git doesn't have much to do. It:

- Determines the parents list — it is one-element and contains the commit pointed by HEAD.
- Has the content of the project already in place — this is the index.
- Determines the author and timestamp, the committer and timestamp.
- Asks for commit message.
- Creates a commit object from the data above, calculates its hash and puts it into the map.
- Moves the current branch (or directly HEAD, in detached HEAD state) to the calculated hash.
- Does nothing with the index!

None of the actions above is long-running — notice, that all blobs and tree objects are already stored in the map.

However, when executing git commit command, you still have to write the commit message.

You can do it this way:

```
git commit -m"Fix some bug"
```

or

```
git commit
```

Git launches the editor and asks you to write down the commit message. Editor defaults to *vi*. After launching the editor you will see something like this:

```
- Please enter the commit message for your changes. Lines starting
- with '-' will be ignored, and an empty message aborts the commit.
-
- information about branch
- changes description (result of the git status command)
-
```

After you close the editor Git reads the saved file and retrieve the commit message from it. If during the edition you decide not to commit, you should close the editor without saving. When using vi, it can be done by typing :cq.

You shouldn't be afraid of creating new commits.

Let's think about committing:

- A commit is project state saved in the map.
- If it was known:
  - how to find the commits in the map and 'use' them,
  - go back to the edition state and start preparing commits once again,

you could go for saving the intermediary states. It would allow you to achieve two seemingly contradictory goals:

- To save the project state often; after some small changes, to facilitate experimenting, etc. You could always resign and go some other way.
- To eventually have several well-organized decent commits, each of which is a finished whole.

How to find commits you have learned in **Reflog**, and you will learn even more in **History reviewing**. About returning to shaping commits again you have learned in **Rebasing — transplanting branches** and you will learn even more in **git reset**. Summing up, you can commit changes pretty often creating 'temporary' commits.

5.5.1. Or maybe work without that much intensity?

The beginner will work like this:

```
git commit -am "Moj komentarz"
```

And they will not care about decent commits or even about saving garbage files. Although, this will not work after creating new files as -a takes into account tracked files only.

But this book is for the intermediate. One of its main purposes is to give the reader knowledge about how to create decent commits, so that they don't have to be ashamed of the commits.

5.5.2. Commit without the index?

The git commit command has the options — e.g. (-a | --all) — that allow the user to commit without previous index shaping. The index might seem not to be used in this case, but in reality it is. The command just modifies the index first, and then 'normally' saves the index as a new commit. In particular, with the (-o | --only) option you can specify which ones from the changed files — in their current state from the working tree — are to be included in the new commit.

5.6. git stash — temporary hiding changes

Documentation: *git stash* [https://git-scm.com/docs/git-stash]

It's not rare that during work, after making series of changes in the working tree and in the index, you need to work with another branch for a while. What should be done with the changes already made in that situation? You can commit them of course. E.g. creating a new branch for a while. But often it's simpler to use git stash command. It stashes the changes in some kind of box, and restores the working tree and the index to the state from HEAD. Changes saved this way can be reapplied later. The situation can repeat before reapplying the hidden changes. Then, you can execute git stash again. Current changes will be stashed in another box.

Git allows to display the current boxes list, to peek at them, restore the saved states and abandon useless boxes.

git stash command has several subcommands. The default subcommand is push.

The simplest session with git stash looks like this:

```
git stash
# do something
```

```
git stash pop
```

what really means:

```
git stash push
# do something
git stash pop
```

That is:

- Hiding changes in a box.
- Doing some work.
- Restoring changes from the last box and deleting it.

E.g.

```
git stash
git pull
git stash pop
```

It looks like a stack, but in fact it's a list. You can restore/delete any element from the list. You can reference the list elements by the stash@{<n>} expression, where <n> equal to 0 means the last box.

The notation suggests that *stash* has its reflog. Indeed — the current list you can display with the git reflog stash command. However, it works differently than with refs — it allows you to display the boxes from the current list only, not any of the deleted ones.

If you don't want to drop the restored box, use git apply [<stash>], instead of git pop [<stash>].

If you use lots of boxes, it could be useful to give them messages (similar to commit messages) git stash push -m <message>. It will be used by git stash list command.

To drop the unnecessary box (without restoring changes saved in it), use git stash drop [<stash>]. To drop all boxes use git stash clear command.

git stash branch <branch-name> [<stash>] command, that is restoring the changes to a new branch, can also be very useful. Well, if a lot of changes were made after git stash push was executed, execution of git stash pop may end up with some merge conflicts to be resolved. It may be easier to execute git stash branch and resolve conflicts between two normal branches, instead of between a branch and a stash box.

By default, git stash push does not save untracked files. It can be forced to do that with the (-u

| --include-untracked) option, or the stronger (-a | --all), which also causes ignored files to be saved.

(-k | --keep-index) is another interesting git stash push option. It makes the command skip the changes added to the index. It allows dividing changes from the working tree into several commits. After adding to the index changes intended to be included in the first commit, execute git stash --keep-index --include-untracked (or git stash -k -u). After that, the working tree content will be identical to the prepared commit. It allows tests to be run against 'upcoming commit'. After creating the commit and executing git stash pop the working tree state goes back to the initial one, but some changes are already included in the commit.

5.7. .gitignore — files you don't want to track

Documentation: *.gitignore* [https://git-scm.com/docs/gitignore]

Often, you don't want some files from the project to be tracked. In this case, the .gitignore file can be used. The file itself can be stored in Git. Its content says what you don't want to track. Each line is a pattern describing the files that Git should ignore.

Sample content of the .gitignore *file*

```
# some directories
log/
target/
build/
# some file patterns
*.log
*~
\#*#
```

As you remember, Git does not track empty directories.

Patterns in .gitignore apply to everyone (so it's good to have it tracked by Git). If you have some additional locally specific patterns, you should put them to the $GIT_DIR/info/exclude.

If the file is already stored in Git, adding it to .gitignore won't cause its removal. It has to be done manually (e.g. git rm --cached <file>).

Tracking of an ignored file can be forced by git add (-f | --forced).

5.8. git checkout — restoring saved state

Documentation: *git checkout* [https://git-scm.com/docs/git-checkout]

5.8.1. Switching between branches

So far we have focused on saving snapshots (project states) in the repository. One does it, to be able to track the history of changes and return to the selected snapshot if needed. Returning to a selected snapshot mainly means to restore it in the working tree. But very often the purpose is to resume development of the graph from this snapshot. Most often it concerns branches and is called switching to the branch or doing a checkout of the branch.

To switch between branches you use:

```
git checkout <branch>
```

After execution, you can resume developing branch <branch>. The <branch> value doesn't have to be a branch. It can be a commit — then the command switches to developing in detached HEAD state.

Similarly, after executing:

```
git checkout -b <new-branch> [<start-point>]
```

you can start developing newly created branch <new-branch> having <start-point> as its tip. <start-point> defaults to HEAD.

Reminder — git commit (most importantly) puts a new commit into the repository. The commit contains the projects state equal to the index. Also, it updates the current branch (or HEAD in detached HEAD state). Checkout works the other way — puts the indicated commit state into the working tree, changes HEAD so that it points to the check-outed branch/commit. But what about the index? Let's think what would be the most practical behaviour.

First, let's notice that:

- Most often a branch is check-outed (not a commit).
- Having a branch, you most often want to resume development of the branch (creating new commits on its tip).

It follows that git checkout should change the index as well, so that after its execution one could instantly resume developing the branch — index agrees with HEAD, so one can proceed normally: to make changes, to add changed files to the index and to commit the changes. The created commit will be a sensible 'continuation' of the branch.

As an exercise one could wonder what would happen if the index hasn't been changed: Content of the index would be as it was before the checkout. You could commit and this way save the previous content in the current branch. Wouldn't it be a strange discontinuation of the branch?

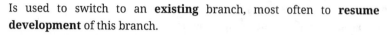

git checkout <branch>

> Is used to switch to an **existing** branch, most often to **resume development** of this branch.

git checkout -b <new-branch> [<start-commit>]

> Is used to switch to a **new** branch pointing to <start-commit> (HEAD by default), most often to **start development** of the created branch.

5.8.2. Switching to the previous branch

git checkout -

> Is used to switch to the previous branch/commit.

This option doesn't exist in the documentation.

5.8.3. Restoring the individual files

Sometimes you want to restore content of a selected file (or files). You can do this with the git checkout command as well.

The file state is restored in both: the working tree and the index. You can restore from any tree, including the index. To do this, you use:

git checkout [<tree-ish>] [--] <pathspec>

> Searches for files compatible with <pathspec> in <tree-ish>, overrides the files in the working tree and in the index.

<tree-ish> defaults to index, thus:

git checkout [--] <pathspec>

> restores files from the index to the working tree.

If the file was removed from the working tree and from the index (with the git rm command), you can restore it with git checkout HEAD -- <file>.

> Checkout of the files is irreversible.

5.8.4. Parameters ambiguity

Notice, that during restoration of the individual files both <tree-ish> and (--) are optional. So, in the command:

```
git checkout foo
```

is foo a branch or a file? If a file, you can use:

```
git checkout -- foo
```

It makes the commands disambiguated. Without -- Git will interpret foo as a branch, if such one exists. So it's safer to use the -- always while restoring individual files.

5.8.5. Untracked files etc.

Checkout can seem to be an easy operation. However, it isn't. Notice, for example, that for the foo.txt file there are four (!) locations of this file:

- the working tree
- the index
- the commit being restored
- HEAD

Not only can the file have different content in any of these locations, but also it can either exist or not in any of them. git checkout has to take it all into account while deciding on existence and the content of the file, both in the working tree and in the index. In particular, merge conflicts (about which soon) can occur.

5.9. git reset — preparing a commit all over again

Documentation: *git reset* [https://git-scm.com/docs/git-reset]

You have already learned how to reorganize commits with git rebase. Now you will learn the git reset command. It operates on HEAD, the index and the working tree. It is kind of similar to git checkout.

One of git reset form is:

```
git reset --hard
```

> *Hard reset* is one of the two operations which can cause irreversible data loss.

In the rest of the chapter we assume that there are no changes in the index before git reset execution.

5.9.1. Reset as undoing the commit to shape it again

Reminder: creation of a commit can be divided into the following phases:

edition of the files in the working tree

> With a text editor, but also with e.g. `git checkout <tree-ish> -- <filespec>`.

stage

> Adding some of the changes made to the index: `git add`, `git rm`, etc.

commit

> Saving the index as a new commit: `git commit`.

`git reset` has three main forms: soft / mixed / hard.

- It undoes the individual stages of commit creation. The 'harder' form of *reset* is used, to the further stage it undoes on the path: **commit → stage → edition**.
- It allows to use the work done (changed files) for the graph development, but starting from a chosen commit (other than the original one). I.e. from the one to which `reset` was done.

In particular `mixed reset` to HEAD is something like: 'Alright, the project state (the working tree) is nice, but I want to organize the commits in a more decent way'.

The basic command version is:

```
git reset [--soft | --mixed | --hard ] [<commit>]
```

Default options are:

- <mode> = *--mixed*
- <commit> = *HEAD*

--soft — undoing commit phase

It moves the current branch to <commit>.
That's it!
Seemingly not much but ... `git commit` can be executed, now. The index hasn't been changed. Therefore, the new commit state will be **the same** as the commit before the reset! This state becomes the next after <commit>. Git as *stupid content tracker* doesn't care where the changes in the index come from. `git commit` command does not ask where the index state came from. It just creates a new commit from the index.

`git reset --soft` not being given <commit> is an empty operation. Being given <commit>, it is the preparation for committing when HEAD points to <commit>.

Personally, I use this very often. Let's say I am working on something and from time to time I am committing. There are already 10 commits. The current state is eligible for creating the final decent commit. I can execute:

```
git reset --soft HEAD~10; git commit
```

and write a beautiful commit message. And it's done — all changes from the 10 commits are included in the final one.

That's correct: after `git reset --soft HEAD~10` execution the current branch is pointing back to the commit to which it was pointing before I started to create new commits. But in the index (and in the working tree) the project state is as it was after making all the changes (all the commits).

In fact, between `reset` and `commit` I often check the changes in the index to make sure that the change made is indeed atomic. If it isn't, I can take the next step and diverge the changes made into several commits.

`--mixed` — undoing commit and stage phases

The `--mixed` options does the same as `--soft` with additional modification of the index so that it contains the exact same project state as `<commit>`.

`git add`; `git commit` can be executed again. The working tree hasn't been changed. To use in the situation as above, but if you want to divide the work done into several commits.

That's correct: after `git reset --mixed HEAD~10` execution the project state in the working tree is as it was **after** making all changes. And the index state is as it was **before** the changes. You can start to add files from the working tree to the index and commit the changes.

`--hard` — undoing phases: commit and stage and edition

The `--hard` options does the same as `--mixed` with additional modification of the working tree so that it contains the same state as the index.

You can start editing the files again, and then execute `git add` and `git commit`. That's correct: after `git reset --hard HEAD~10` execution all changes made disappeared from both the index and the working tree. The current branch points back to the original commit.

5.9.2. Reset of the individual files — restoring in the index

Similarly to `git checkout`, `git reset` has its own version operating on the individual files.

```
git reset [<tree-ish>] [--] <pathspec>
```

This `git reset` form operates on the individual files, so it does not change HEAD (HEAD points to a commit, which is a whole snapshot, not any individual files).

`--soft` option makes no sense, as it operates on HEAD **only**.

--hard option should change the index and the working tree (still not touching HEAD, as an operation on some files only, not on the whole commit). Which means it would do the same as git checkout -- <pathspec>, so it doesn't make much sense either.

At the end, git reset⎵⎵<pathspec> does not have the options **soft** / **mixed** / **hard**. It is just **mixed** version, not changing HEAD. Thus:

> git reset [<tree-ish>] [--] <pathspec> puts contents of the specified files in their versions from <tree-ish> into the index.
> In other words: restores the files contents from <tree-ish> into the index.

In particular, as <tree-ish> defaults to HEAD:

> git reset [--] <pathspec> puts the specified files from the current commit into the index.
> So it is undoing git add of the individual files.

5.10. git checkout vs git reset

One can ask: As git checkout and git reset --hard both change HEAD, the index and the working tree, are they not the same? There is one subtle, yet important difference between them:

hard reset Does not modify HEAD itself, but the branch pointed by HEAD.

checkout Modifies HEAD itself, switching it to another branch.
It doesn't modify the branch itself — neither the original, nor the new one.

The above illustrates intentions of the two commands:

hard reset Clears the foreground and prepares for resuming the development

- of the current branch
- starting from the indicated commit.

checkout Clears the foreground and prepares for resuming the development

- of the indicated branch
- from its tip.

Table 1. changes made by the commands

command	changes HEAD/branch	changes index	changes working tree
git reset --soft	branch	no	no

command	changes HEAD/branch	changes index	changes working tree
git reset --mixed	branch	yes	no
git reset --hard	branch	yes	yes
git checkout	HEAD	yes	yes

5.11. Merging in details, merge conflicts

All commands reconciling the changes between different project states, that is:

- creating new commits on the basis of others already existing:
    - merge
    - revert
    - rebase
    - cherry-pick
- restoring the project state in the working tree/the index:
    - checkout
    - stash pop
    - reset --mixed

can encounter a problem.

The same file might have been changed in two different ways. Sometimes these changes can be reconciled. For instance, if the first change was made at the beginning of a file, and the second one at the end of the file, the final file state can include both changes. However, the case when the changes were made in the same part of the file, cannot be merged that easily. They are called *merge conflicts*, Git asks the user to *resolve the conflicts*.

Conflict resolving is basically deciding how the final file should look like and communicating it to Git (e.g. with the git add command). Git itself:

- Tries to help: it joins the changes if there are no conflicts.
- Lets the user decide how to deal with the files having merge conflicts.

For programmers
The fact that Git managed to merge changes from two branches without any trouble, doesn't mean that the result is correct. For example, let's say that the first change deletes a method and all its usages but the second one adds new usages of this method. As a result the method will disappear still being in use and the final result won't compile. It could be even worse — the file and even the whole project will compile but some subtle semantic errors can arise.

5.11.1. Starting, stopping and continuing

It is a good practice not to execute the commands above when — either in the index or in the working tree — there are any uncommitted changes. Usually Git will remind the user about this. git stash can be used to hide the changes (see *git stash*).

Conflicts resolving can be not an easy task. Sometimes one has to give up and start once again from the beginning. Individual commands have the --abort option, which serves for that purpose. There is also the --quit option. This is similar to --abort but without undoing the changes made to the index in the meantime.

Quite often conflicts resolving has to be done in several steps. This is why the commands have the --continue and the --skip options.

Continuing options for the individual commands

```
git merge (--continue | --abort | --quit)
git revert (--continue | --skip | --abort | --quit)
git rebase (--continue | --skip | --abort | --quit | --edit-todo | --show-current-patch)
git cherry-pick (--continue | --skip | --abort | --quit)
```

5.11.2. Merge sides — *ours* and *theirs*

In the *git merge* chapter three-way merge and merge base were described.
Reminder: most often what is merged are two branches (their tips).

Assuming that:

- master is the main branch, pointing to the commit X,
- feature is the branch being merged, pointing to the commit Y,

merging feature to master looks like this:

```
git checkout master
git merge feature
```

If everything goes smoothly, a new commit with the two-element parents list: < X, Y > will be created.

Merging two commits, X and Y, has three sides (three commits).

ours, LOCAL The main side (X).

theirs, REMOTE The side being merged (Y).

<table>
<tr><td>**merge base, BASE**</td><td>The merge base is the youngest common ancestor of X and Y (a commit).</td></tr>
</table>

merge base, BASE   The merge base is the youngest common ancestor of X and Y (a commit).

In other words: the place of divergence of the main side and the being merged side (git merge-base X Y). Let's assume that this is commit B.

5.11.3. Commits, trees, blobs

Notice, that the merging sides are **commits**. I.e. the whole snapshots. However, in the merge process itself, the **individual files**, one after another, are taken into account. Merge conflict can occur during merging each individual file.

Notice also, that there **are no** conflicts on the **trees** (directories) level. It is all about comparing versions of the individual files (**blobs** from base, ours and theirs). Adding/deleting a file (appearing, disappearing of the blob; do not confuse with the empty blob) is treated as a special kind of its modification.

Merging a file is checking whether the file has changed in both ours and theirs sides in reference to base. Or if just in one, or maybe it hasn't changed at all. If it has changed in at most one side, as a merge result this changed version is taken. If it changed in both, it has to be analysed further and potentially a merge conflict can occur.

5.11.4. Merging in the index

During merging the index and Git's content-addressable map are intensively used:

- Index is displayed with:
    - git ls-files (-s | --stage) displays enriched information about files from the index.
    - git ls-files (-u | --unmerged) limits to the unmerged files, forces --stage.
- The mysterious zero occurring with the files is so-called stage number.
  0 means that the file (with the content identified by the hash) is merged and ready to be saved in the next commit.
- During merging the file can have the following stage number values: 1, 2 and 3. If any of them occurs, the file isn't merged yet.
- For each file occurring in the X, Y or B, for these X, Y, B in which the file occurs, the versions of this file are put into the index:

    - 1 for B, base
    - 2 for X, ours
    - 3 for Y, theirs

  For example, if the file was added by the commit X, only version 2 of the file will occur:

- For each file Git attempts to calculate its merged content. If it succeeds, it is noted as 'reduction' of the file to version 0 and all other versions of this file are removed from the index.

- Files, which weren't reduced to version 0, are conflicts.
- Resolving (by the user) a conflict of a file causes its reduction to 0 (and deletion of its other versions) in the index or its complete removal from the index (when the user decides to delete the file).

The reduction isn't very complicated. There are three versions (1 - base, 2 - ours, 3 - theirs) of the file content — remember: non-existence of the version in the index means non-existence of the file in the corresponding side (commit). Git checks how base changes in the branches ours and theirs.

To execute the reductions above Git doesn't have to compare contents of the individual files. It simply compares the hashes. And those are stored in the index!

Reduction can be done instantly (without comparing the contents), in the following situations:

- No changes: 1, 2 and 3 are the same — reduction to the original version.
- The same changes are done in both branches (2 == 3) — reduction to the modified version. In particular:
  - Adding the file — there is no 1, both 2 and 3 occurs with the same content.
  - Deleting the file — there is 1, there is neither 2 nor 3.
- There is a change, but just in one branch (either 1 == 3 or 3 == 1) — reduction to the modified version. In particular:
  - Adding the file — there is no 1, there is only 2 or there is only 3.
- Change in one branch, deleting in the other (e.g. there is 1, 2 is missing, 1 != 3) — **conflict!**

Situation when Git can't reduce instantly means that the changes are done both in 2 and 3 and they differ. It covers the following cases:

- Change of the file in one branch, deleting in the other — **conflict!**
- Adding file in both branches, in each with the different content.
- Change of the file in both branches, with the different content in each of them.

Two last cases are not obvious. Git tries to take a look into particular contents of the file and reconcile these changes.

Changes between 1 and 2 and between 1 and 3 are diverged to the hunks. If each of the individual hunk has changed in one branch only, all changes, hunk by hunk, are applied to 1. Then the file becomes reduced to 0.
However, if any hunk has changed in both branches — **conflict!**

In **Versions of blobs and trees**, it was described how the content of the file in the specific version can be displayed.

5.11.5. Conflicts resolving

If there is any unsolved merge conflict — i.e. a not reduced file in the index — Git won't allow the user to execute `git commit`. Before that all conflicts in all files must be solved. And that must be done by the user.

Even in merge conflict case, there is no partially-merged version of the file in the index:

- Either Git has managed to merge the file versions, or the user has solved the conflict — there is only version 0 in the index,
- or not — there in no version 0 in the index, but some of original versions: 1, 2 and/or 3.

For each file, for which a conflict has occurred, several files are saved in the working tree:

- File version with the marked conflicted hunks — under the original file name.
- File versions corresponding to the individual merge sides — under the names with appropriate suffixes.

The files are important; they are used by the tools helping with conflicts resolving. It is often a good idea to use those tools.

 For the files changed in reference to base both in ours and theirs, *merge conflicts* can occur. Every single conflict must be solved by the user. It is a good idea to use graphical tools helping with conflicts resolving.

5.11.6. Merging strategy

Git can take different merge approaches, called *merge strategies*. The description above refers to the default behaviour. Some merge strategies can take their own options modifying the strategy behaviour. The strategy can be chosen with the **-s** option, and options for the strategy with the **-X** option.

For example, the default strategy can be given ours or theirs as -X option. It will cause the conflicts to be solved automatically — the side pointed by the option wins.

Description of the merging strategies can be found in the documentation **merge strategies** *[https://git-scm.com/docs/git-merge#_merge_strategies]*.

5.12. `git rerere` — solving the same conflict all over again

Documentation: **git rerere** [https://git-scm.com/docs/git-rerere]

Sometimes you will have to resolve the same conflict many times. `git rerere` (**Reuse recorded resolution**) command can help.

6. History reviewing

6.1. `git log` — history reviewing

Documentation: *git log* [https://git-scm.com/docs/git-log]

```
git log [<options>] [<revision-range>] [[--] <path>…]
```

The command allows to review the commit history. There are so many options that another book could be written about this command. Only some of the options will be described or mentioned in this chapter.

\<revision-range\>	Display the history of commits from *\<revision-range\>*. See ***Commit ranges***. Defaults to HEAD.
[--] \<path\>...	Limit the list of commits to these only, which changes any file from \<path\>…. As usual, -- is required when the path is ambiguous. E.g. when *foo* is both a branch name and a file name.
(-g | --walk-reflogs)	Use reflog instead of the ancestor relationship.

6.1.1. Filtering the results

Options limiting the displayed commits list are compatible with the options of the `git rev-list` command (see *git rev-list* [https://git-scm.com/docs/git-rev-list]). They are used before sorting and formatting the result.

(-\<n\> \| -n \<n\> \| --max-count=\<n\>)

The maximum count of commits to be displayed.

--skip=\<n\>

Skip \<n\> commits.

by the branches/tags/remote repositories

--[branches \| tags \| remotes][=\<pattern\>]
--glob=\<glob-patterns\>
--exclude=\<glob-patterns\>

--author=\<pattern\>, --committer=\<pattern\>

Several values can be given.

by timestamp

--since-as-filter, --since, --after, --until, --before

`--since-as-filter` can be especially useful while working with rebase. `--since` stops after reaching the first old commit, `--since-as-filter` checks all commits and then filters the old ones.

by the ancestors amount

--min-parents=<n>, --max-parents=<n>, --no-min-parents, --no-max-parents

In particular skipping or taking into account merge commits only: (**--no-merges, --merges**).

by the commit message

Many options, regular expressions etc.

logical expressions

--not, --all

6.1.2. Sorting

Sorting is done after the commits have been filtered.

The youngest commits are displayed at the top, then their parents and so on.

--reverse   Display in reverse order.

6.1.3. Graph

--graph   Display the result as a graph.

6.1.4. Formatting the results

Presentation of commits

There are several predefined formats and custom ones can be defined as well. Predefined values are: *oneline, short, medium, full, fuller, reference, email, raw.*

--abbrev-commit	Shorten the commit ID.
--date=<format>	Use given date format.
--relative-date	Abbreviation for `--date=relative`.
--oneline	Abbreviation for `--pretty=oneline --abbrev -commit`.

--format=<format>	Defaults to *medium*.
--pretty[=<format>]	The available forms list is described in the documentation, see ***pretty formats** [https://git-scm.com/docs/git-log#_pretty_formats]*.
--source	Show from which tip (leaf) the commit was reached.

Presentation of the differences between the commits

Documentation: ***git diff*** [https://git-scm.com/docs/git-diff]

There are lots of options allowing to display the information not only about commits but also about differences between them. By default, the differences are not displayed.

Options defining way of displaying the changes applied by the commits are compatible with the options of the `git diff` command.

--summary	Show the information about new and about deleted files.
--shortstat	Show the summary of the changes amount.
--stat	Show the names of files changed by the commit along with the statistics of changes.
--name-only	Show the names of files changed by the commit.
--name-status	Show the names of the files changed by the commit along with the kind of the changes.
--follow	Allows to track the changes of the file in spite of a change of its name. Works for one file only.
(-M[<n>] | --find-renames[=<n>])	Allows to change policy of file name changes detection.

6.2. `git shortlog` — summary of the history

Documentation: ***git shortlog*** [https://git-scm.com/docs/git-shortlog]

Allows to display the summary of the changes history grouped by the author or the committer.

Part II: Git remotely

The first part of the book was about working with a local repository, i.e. about growing the commit graph.

The second part will treat about cooperating with the remote repositories, i.e. about sharing (downloading and sending) parts of the graph from/to other repositories. This part is surprisingly short. It turns out that most of the hard work is local.

7. Remote repository

7.1. `git remote` — remote repositories

Documentation: ***git remote*** [https://git-scm.com/docs/git-remote]

The possibility to work locally without network connection is very comfortable. With Git, having the whole project history locally, you can do almost everything without internet connection:

- To switch between branches.
- To develop the commit graph (many branches).
- To review the history.
- To make backups.
  E.g., copying the `.git` directory to an external disk. This form of doing backups might be primitive, but still every backup done this way contains the **whole history** of the project.

The only thing missing is the possibility to cooperate with the others, i.e.:

- Getting their work effects, which simply means adding their commits to the graph.
  It can be done with the `git fetch` command.
- Sharing the work done with the others, which simply means putting new commits to their repositories.
  It can be done with the `git push` command.

To be able to do that, you have to work with at least two repositories:

- yours, called a *local repository*
- others, called a *remote repositories*

Most often just one remote repository is in use.

Being *distributed* system means, that from the remote repository's point of view, it is your repository which is remote and the remote is local.

For example, the primitive form of doing backup mentioned above, can be done differently:

- Initiate a Git repository on an external disk.
- Define your repository as a remote repository there.
- On that disk, download with the `git fetch` command.

Or:

- In your repository, define a remote repository as the one from the external disk.
- Push to it with the `git push` command.

Let's assume that your repository is in the /home/me/git/samplerepo dir, and that the external disk is in the /home/mnt/backup dir.

Primitive copy with downloading on the external disk

```
# setup the backup and fetch the first backup
cd /home/mnt/backup
mkdir samplerepo
cd samplerepo
git clone /home/me/git/samplerepo./git
# backup changes
git fetch
```

Primitive copy with pushing to the external disk

```
# setup the backup
cd /home/mnt/backup
mkdir samplerepo
cd /home/me/git/samplerepo
git init
git remote add backup /home/mnt/backup/samplerepo/.git
# backup a new branch, let's say foo
git branch -u backup/foo foo
git push backup
```

The downloading version is the simpler one. Pushing version gives more control over what you want to put into the backup.

In practice the peer-to-peer (co)operation is a rare way of work. Most often one deals with one main (central) repository, so-called *source of truth*, and many secondary repositories (local copies). Each programmer has their own local copy (secondary repository). Any changes from the colleagues aren't downloaded directly to it; no changes are shared directly from it. The programmers fetch the commits from the main repository (put there by colleagues) and push their (produced locally) commits to it.

This central repository on the server is usually managed by some software providing various additional features, such as:

- Authorization. Git doesn't offer any authorizations itself.
- Forcing the decided `workflow`.
  E.g. users to add their commits to branch `master`, have to create some other branch and then merge it. In addition, to be merged, the branch must meet the established code standards.
- Code review.
- Mechanisms for running tests, build and CI/CD pipelines.

Popular solutions are:

- GitHub
- GibLab
- BitBucket
- Gerrit

Working with a remote repositories means:

- Fetching commits from it with the `git fetch` command.
- Pushing commits to it with the `git push` command.

7.1.1. Defining the remote repository

To define a `remote repository`, two things must be given:

name   I.e. how this repository will be referenced locally.

address   I.e. how the repository will be reached by Git.

It can be done by:

```
git remote add <name> <repo>
```

command, e.g.

```
git remote add origin https://github.com/spring-projects/spring-framework.git
```

Remote repository name

The most common remote repository name is *origin*. The reason for it is: most often the local repository is created not by initiation of a directory as a Git project (`git init`), but by cloning a remote repository (`git clone`, will be described soon). *origin* is the default name of the remote repository given during cloning. But you can name it otherwise. The situation is similar to the standard branch name — *master*.

`origin` is the default name used for the entity named **remote repository**. This name is used as default by:
`git clone`, `git fetch` and `git push` commands.

Address of the remote repository

Address of the remote repository usually point to some repository on a server (like GitHub). But it can point to the repository on your colleague's computer or on your local computer as well. In the last case, it is just the path to the appropriate *.git* directory!

7.1.2. Cooperation of the repositories

A Git repository is a graph of commits. Therefore, the remote repository can be seen as a pointer to another graph.

So now you have several graphs of commits. One of them is special — that is your local one.

To find out which remote repositories are seen by your local, you can execute:

```
git remote -v
```

Usually the output will look out like this:

```
origin   https://github.com/spring-projects/spring-framework.git (fetch)
origin   https://github.com/spring-projects/spring-framework.git (push)
```

Fetch and push seem to be somehow separated which suggests, that the remote repository can point to two graphs! Indeed, you can fetch commits from one repository and push to another one. It will be some optimization, probably. Pushes are done to the main repository but fetches are done from a *mirror server*.

A question appears: **How do the graphs cooperate?**
In other words: **How do the graphs share subgraphs?**

The power of repository implementation as a graph/content-addressable map shines here brightly. The graph in which the vertices are objects (commits) and the edges are coded in these objects as list of commits-parents. All objects are immutable. All objects are stored in the content-addressable map.

Cooperation is just sending (copying) Git objects between the graphs. As you remember, there are four kinds of Git objects: commits, trees, blobs and tags. If you ask Git to send the commit between two graphs, it will send not only the commit object, but all objects 'used' by the commit:

- trees and blobs added to the map by this commit

- all ancestors
- trees and blobs added by the ancestors

To check, whether an object needs to be sent, Git just has to check if its hash exists in the target database (content-addressable map).

In practise after adding a commit there will not be many objects to be sent because the target repository will already contain:

- many of previous commits (ancestors)
- many of the trees — corresponding to directories in which nothing has changed
- many of the blobs — corresponding to the files which haven't change

This is how the cooperation between the graphs looks like. Of course, sending subgraphs between repositories has to be easy and comfortable. The situation is sort of similar to work with a local repository. Namely, what eases work with a local repository is decorating the graph with refs, especially with branches (tips of the branches?!). What eases work with a remote repository is decorating the graph with another kind of branches, and then relating branches of the two kinds. Branches of the new kind are called *remote-tracking branches*. They will be discussed in the next chapter.

7.2. Branches: local, remote, tracking, remote-tracking and upstreams

There are several kinds of branches:

- *local branches*, those are **normal** branches — We have been working with them so far. They can be displayed with the `git branch` command.
- *remote branches*, those are branches in remote repositories. Let's notice, that they are local branches in the remote repository, and only from our repository's point of view they are remote.
  Actually, this isn't any special kind of branch. Usage of the *local/remote* term just allows us to distinguish if a 'normal' branch is from the local repository or rather from any remote one.
  The remote branches can be displayed with the `git ls-remote [<remote>]` command. The result is a little bit richer than the one for the local branches.
- *remote-tracking branches*, those are representations of remote branches in the local repository.
  Such branches correspond to the remote branches with the same names and store the values (commit IDs) of appropriate remote branches. The values come from the last synchronization time with the remote repository. Those branches are not created explicitly! Remote-tracking branches can be displayed with `git branch -a` command. They are the ones like `remotes/<remote>/<branch>`. So, such a branch is identified by two names:
  - the name of the remote repository,
  - the name of the branch in this remote repository.

- *tracking branches*, those are local branches related to some remote-tracking branches. The remote-tracking branch plays the role of *upstream* in this relationship. Similar to remote branches *tracking branch* isn't a **name** of a special kind of branch. It is a **statement**, that an upstream has been set for this branch. Each local branch can become or cease to be a tracking branch, because its upstream can always be set or unset

There are two main kinds of branches:

- *normal branch*
  - It is identified by `refs/heads/<branch>`.
  - It can be a branch in a remote repository (i.e. identified by `refs/heads/<branch>` in the remote repository), not in the local one. It is called then a *remote branch*. In case of a local repository it is called a **local branch**.
  - It can have an upstream (a remote-tracking branch) set, which allows it to cooperate with the remote branch.

    It is called then a *tracking branch*.

  - It is changing during the graph development, i.e. during execution of commands: `commit`, `checkout`, `reset`, `merge`, `rebase` and `revert`.
- *remote-tracking branch*
  - It is identified by `refs/remotes/<remote>/<branch>`.
  - It stores the value of a remote branch.
  - It can be an upstream of a normal branch (making the normal branch tracking).
  - It is changing only during exchanging the subgraphs with the remote repositories, i.e. during execution of commands: `fetch` and `push`.

upstream is a property of a local branch establishing a connection between this branch and a remote branch.
The values of upstreams are remote-tracking branches.

It's high time for some experiments.

1. Let's try to switch to a remote-tracking branch:

```
git checkout remotes/origin/<somebranch>
```

We are in detached HEAD state, in the commit pointed by `remotes/origin/<somebranch>`.

Let's go back:

```
git checkout -
```

2. Let's do it otherwise.

```
git checkout origin/<somebranch>
```

Detached HEAD again. Git has found <somebranch> in remotes.
Let's go back:

```
git checkout -
```

3. Third time lucky:

```
git checkout <somebranch>
```

Something different! Git said:

```
Switched to branch 'release'
Your branch is up-to-date with 'origin/release'.
```

```
git branch
```

A new branch has been created:

```
git branch -vv
```

```
* <somebranch> 1867d2b [<remote>/<somebranch>] <commit message>
```

Git found the branch <somebranch> among the remote-tracking branches remotes/<remote>/*. On that basis Git created branch <somebranch> and set its:

- value to the commit pointed by remotes/<remote>/<somebranch>,
- upstream to branch remotes/<remote>/<somebranch>.

This new local branch <somebranch> is ready to cooperate with remote branch <somebranch> from repository <remote>. These branches are related, by the upstream of the local branch. The value of this upstream is remote-tracking branch remotes/<remote>/<somebranch>.

For example, let's say that you are co-working with others developing branch foo.

Local branch foo can be related to some remote branch, e.g. origin/foo, by setting the upstream.

The intention is clear: You want to share your work — developed in foo — with others, by sending new commits to the remote repository. From there, they can fetch those commits. If someone has pushed their commits to that repository, you can fetch them to your local repository.

7.2.1. Setting an upstream explicitly

Switching to a remote branch creates a local branch and sets its upstream. However, sometimes you may want to manage the upstreams manually.

Setting the upstream explicitly

```
git checkout -b <somebranch> <remote>/<somebranch>^{commit} ①
git branch --set-upstream-to=<remote>/<somebranch> ②
```

① Creating the local branch pointing to the same commit as the remote-tracking branch. Without setting the upstream.

② Setting the upstream.

The upstream can be unset with:

```
git branch --unset-upstream <branch>
```

command. While the remote-tracking branches are not removed manually, it can be done either with a special command, or during fetching the changes from the remote repository.

8. Fetching and pushing

8.1. git fetch — fetching subgraphs from a remote repository

Documentation: ***git fetch*** [https://git-scm.com/docs/git-fetch]

In this chapter you will learn to fetch commits from a remote repository.

Reminder: a branch is just a non-symbolic ref pointing to some commit. Sometimes we say that the given commit is the tip of the branch or the *value* of the branch.

8.1.1. Fetching a single branch

You know, that the value of local branch foo changes during execution of git commit command. It also changes during execution of the following commands: checkout, reset (mixed i hard), merge, rebase, revert.
But when and how does the value of remote-tracking branch origin/foo changes?

Let's assume that new commits have appeared in the branch foo in the remote repository. Which means, that branch foo has changed in the remote repository (where the branch is local). Which means it points to another commit than the corresponding remote-tracking branch in your repository points to.

During execution of git fetch origin foo the following things happen:

- Checking foo's value in the remote repository (what a commit it is) and writing this information to .git/FETCH_HEAD.

- If the commit is absent in the local repository, it gets fetched from the remote repository. The commit itself and **all** necessary objects, that is the whole history of the commit.

- In the local repository remote-tracking branch origin/foo gets moved to the commit written in .git/FETCH_HEAD.

That's it! Your local graph has grown, and branch origin/foo points to the same commit as foo in the remote repository again.
Notice, that local branch foo has not changed!

A real example:

```
git fetch origin main
```

```
remote: Enumerating objects: 1449, done.
remote: Counting objects: 100% (1137/1137), done.
remote: Compressing objects: 100% (442/442), done.
remote: Total 1449 (delta 501), reused 1079 (delta 484), pack-reused 312
Receiving objects: 100% (1449/1449), 529.77 KiB | 11.52 MiB/s, done.
Resolving deltas: 100% (517/517), completed with 144 local objects.
From https://github.com/spring-projects/spring-framework
 * branch                  main         -> FETCH_HEAD
   7700570253..a6cd8a78e2  main         -> origin/main
```

Let's see, what the individual lines mean:

```
 * branch                  main       -> FETCH_HEAD
```

Value of the remote branch main is written to FETCH_HEAD.

```
7700570253..a6cd8a78e2  main        -> origin/main
```

```
 remote-tracking branch `origin/main` pointed to commit 7700570253`,
and points to `a6cd8a78e2`, now.
```

- Lines with
  - Enumerating — Git enumerates objects to be fetched.
  - Counting, ···, Resolving — Git fetches the enumerated objects, compressing them for the time of transport.

If there was nothing to fetch, the message would be much shorter:

```
From https://github.com/spring-projects/spring-framework
 * branch              main        -> FETCH_HEAD
```

How long does such a fetch last? You can experiment, fetching some repository, e.g.

```
git init
git remote add origin https://github.com/spring-projects/spring-framework
time git fetch origin main
time git checkout main
git log --pretty=oneline | wc -l
```

The result is not bad, as for such a large repository:

Several seconds to fetch the full project history

```
remote: Enumerating objects: 582278, done.
remote: Counting objects: 100% (555/555), done.
remote: Compressing objects: 100% (351/351), done.
remote: Total 582278 (delta 111), reused 449 (delta 87), pack-reused 581723
Receiving objects: 100% (582278/582278), 158.27 MiB | 17.29 MiB/s, done.
Resolving deltas: 100% (285908/285908), done.
From https://github.com/spring-projects/spring-framework
 * branch              main        -> FETCH_HEAD
 * [new branch]        main        -> origin/main

real    0m15,718s
user    0m18,050s
sys     0m2,499s
```

Half second to switch to a branch

```
Branch 'main' set up to track remote branch 'main' from 'origin' by rebasing.
Switched to a new branch 'main'

real    0m0,553s
user    0m0,346s
sys     0m0,203s
```

Repository contains over 26000 commits

```
git rev-list --all --count
26162
```

After `git fetch <remote> <branch>` execution, in the local repository:

- The value of the **remote-tracking branch** `<remote>/<branch>` is set to the same commit as the value of the remote branch `<branch>`.
- The whole history of the commit (the subgraph) is contained in the local repository.

`git fetch` is a 'safe' operation. It modifies only:

- the local repository — adding new object to it,
- the remote-tracking branches,

and it does **nothing**:

- in the working tree,
- with the local branches (even with the tracking ones).

In addition, all tags reachable from the tip of branch `<branch>` are fetched.

8.1.2. Fetching many branches

You don't have to specify the branch you want to fetch.

```
git fetch <remote>
```

is enough. Git will do a bit more, it:

- Fetches all new remote branches and creates remote-tracking branches for them.
- Updates all remote-tracking branches.

- Fetches tags reachable from the remote-tracking branches.

Usually, you don't have to specify the remote you want to fetch from. You can type:

```
git fetch
```

How does Git know which remote repository should be taken into account? There are two options:

- If the current branch is a tracking one, the remote of the upstream is used.
- Otherwise, the name *origin* is used.

The changes from all remote repositories can also be fetched at once:

```
git fetch --all
```

In fact the above examples are the most common cases. In reality the Git world is much richer and a simple git fetch uses various configurable settings. As usual, the defaults allow the user not to care too much about it.

8.1.3. General form of fetching

In general, git fetch command looks like this:

```
git fetch [<options>] [<repository> [<refspec>···]]
```

Instead of simple <remote> more general <repository> can be used. Instead of <branch> a <refspec> list can be used.

We will go back to that after describing **repository** and **refspec**. In particular, the following versions of the fetch command will be described:

```
git fetch <remote> <remote-branch>:<local-branch>
```

8.1.4. Deleting withered branches

A remote branch can be deleted, but it does not mean that the remote-tracking branch, which tracks the branch, will also disappear. It won't. Even after execution of git fetch. The only thing done when fetching is noticing in the local repository that the corresponding remote branch does not exist anymore. One could call a remote-tracking branch without its remote counterpart: dangling (as it is a ref) or withered (as it is a branch).

You can make `git fetch` delete withered branches this way:

```
git fetch -p
```

or without fetching with the command:

```
git remote prune <remote>
```

Notice, that both commands have to connect to the remote repository to see which branches were there deleted.

8.1.5. Useful options

--dry-run	Do not execute. Just show what is about to happen.
(-a | --all)	Fetch from all remotes.
--depth=<depth>	Do not fetch the whole history but to the given depth only. There exist also several similar options.
(-p | --prune)	Delete the remote-tracking branches which don't have the corresponding remote branches anymore.
(-P | --prune-tags)	Delete all tags absent in the remote repository. Including these which were created only locally!
(-n | --no-tags)	Do not fetch the tags.
(-t | --tags)	Fetch all tags, even not reachable from any branch. This option can be useful when the branch was deleted but some tags, not reachable anymore, are still relevant. Normally, only reachable tags are fetched.

> ℹ️ `git fetch` modifies the remote-tracking branches **only**. It does not modify the local branches unless forced!

8.2. `git push` — sending subgraphs to a remote repository

Documentation: ***git push*** [https://git-scm.com/docs/git-push]

The `git push` command works similar to `git fetch`, but the data is sent in the reverse direction. Let's note, that the situation isn't totally symmetrical. In most cases:

1. Remote repository plays the role of *source of truth*.

2. Remote repository doesn't have any equivalent of remote-tracking branches.

3. Remote repository is kind of server in client-server architecture. To call the server, client has to know it (what's done by defining the remote). But the server doesn't know the clients it serves. Pushing modifies remote branches directly (not any remote-tracking ones).

4. Without any parameters given, `git push` by default pushes the current branch **only**. `git fetch` fetches **everything**, using the current branch only to specify where it should fetch from. It makes sense:

   ◦ During fetching you don't know how many changes have been made in the remote repository. But everything that has been changed there might be interesting as getting up to date with the source of truth.

   ◦ In opposite, you most likely want to push the current branch only. Other branches, even locally modified, might not be ready to be pushed. Probably, you also have some 'private' branches, which you don't want to push at all.

Notice, that both `git fetch` and `git push` are most often used when the current branch is a tracking branch. Both commands use the upstream to specify **from where/to where** (remote repository) and **what** should be fetched/pushed. If the branch is not a tracking one, *origin* is used. `git fetch` fetches everything. `git push` pushes the current branch.

8.2.1. Pushing a single branch

If the current branch is a tracking branch, pushing it is just as simple as:

```
git push
```

Both remote repository and the name of the remote branch is taken from the upstream.

Any branch can be pushed, even non-tracking.

```
git push <remote> <branch>
```

8.2.2. Pushing with creation of a remote-tracking branch

Setting upstream when pushing is an often used option:

```
git push (-u | --set-upstream) <remote> <branch>
```

For example, when after one has created the local branch <branch>, it is time to publish it. The purpose is to configure the branch for further cooperation with its counterpart in <remote> at once. More precisely: beside modification of the remote repository, the remote-tracking branch is created in the local repository. Subsequently, the remote-tracking branch is set as the upstream of branch <branch>. Thus, during next pushes branch <branch> will have an upstream, so simple `git push` will be enough.

8.2.3. General form of pushing

Similar to `git fetch`, general `git push` command form is:

```
git push [<options>] [<repository> [<refspec>···]]
```

Instead of simple <remote> more general <repository> can be used. Instead of <branch> a <refspec> list can be used.

We will go back to that after describing **repository** and **refspec**.

In particular, we will describe commands like this:

```
git push <remote> <commit>:<branch>
```

8.2.4. Deleting the remote branch

A remote branch can be deleted by:

```
git push (-d | --delete) <remote> <branch>
```

or in the old-school way:

```
git push <remote> :<branch>
```

8.2.5. *Non-fast-forward* changes

Pushing *non-fast-forward* changes might not be the best idea. You have to know what you are doing, especially when your colleagues are not expecting such changes. It is justified if the team uses rebase instead of merge. It cannot be avoided then and everyone is aware and ready for it.

Use the **(-f | --force)** option to push *non-fast-forward* changes.

8.2.6. On the remote repository side

As mentioned, remote (central) repository normally has no equivalent of remote-tracking branches. One pushes directly to remote branches. Moreover, although you usually want to fetch everything, the remote repository may reject the changes being pushed (e.g. the changes don't meet the established standards, workflow). Some rules may be enforced by configuration or hooks [https://git-scm.com/docs/githooks] mechanism. Sending additional information — by using the (-o <string> | --push-option=<string>) option — can be also useful. It allows the remote repository to do something additional. For example, creating a merge request in GitLab can look like this:

```
git push -o merge_request.create -o merge_request.target=master
```

8.2.7. Useful options

(-n | --dry-run)	Do not execute. Just show what is about to happen.
(-f | --force)	Force acceptance of non-fast-forward changes on the remote repository.
(-u | --set-upstream)	Set the upstream.
(-d | --delete)	Delete from the remote repository.
(-o | --push-option)=<string>	Send additional information. It will be available for `pre-receive` and `post-receive` hooks.
--follow-tags	Push also tags reachable from the commits being pushed.

8.3. `git pull` — both `fetch` and `merge`/`rebase` at once

Documentation: *git pull* [https://git-scm.com/docs/git-pull]

`git pull <remote> <branch>` does two things:

- `git fetch` (with the same parameters as `git pull` was called),
- reconciliation of fetched changes — `git merge FETCHED_HEAD` or `git rebase FETCHED_HEAD`, based on configuration.

Similar to `git fetch`, the general `git pull` form can be:

```
git pull [<options>] [<repository> [<refspec>···]]
```

where `<repository>` and `<refspec>` work the same way as with `git fetch`. In particular, the default values are:

<repository>   Remote repository of the upstream or `origin` if the current branch is not tracking.

<refspec>   Based on the configuration and the upstream.

Most often, i.e. when the current branch is a tracking branch, there is nothing to wonder about — `git pull` will do the job. However, in more complicated cases it's better to run `git fetch` first, and `git merge`/`rebase` or anything you need afterward.

8.4. `git clone` — creating a secondary repository

Documentation: ***git clone*** [https://git-scm.com/docs/git-clone]

```
git clone [options] [--] <repository> [<directory>]
```

The `git clone` command does something like this:

```
# error if <directory> exists and is not empty
mkdir <directory> # if needed
cd <directory>
git remote add origin <repository>
git fetch
git pull
```

<repository>

Address of the repository to be cloned. See ***repository***.

<directory>

The directory to which the repository will be cloned. This defaults to the repository name, but other name can be indicated. If the directory does not exist, it gets created. If it exists, it has to be empty.

Repository created like this is already configured to cooperate with the cloned one. Usually local repository plays the role of a secondary repository, for which the cloned remote repository is source of truth.

The created repository can be special provided an appropriate option is used.

bare   Without working tree, useful on the server.

shared   Do not use it.

These are special cases, not covered by this book.

8.4.1. Useful options

(-n | --dry-run)   Do not execute. Just show what is about to happen.

(-o | --origin) <name>   Explicitly indicating the name of the remote repository.

(-b | — branch) <name>   Explicitly indicating what should be fetched.

--separate-git-dir=<git-dir> If you want to have repositories in one place and working trees in another.

--no-tags   Do not fetch the tags.

8.4.2. Other interesting options

Options below can be used to accelerate the cloning process. For example, it could play role on a CI server, where normally only one specific commit is needed.

--depth <depth>   Do not fetch the whole history, only to indicated depth.

--single-branch   Fetch one branch only.

Part III: Supplements

9. Repositories configurations

9.1. *refspec* — mapping between local and remote repositories

This topic is very complicated, and it will be just slightly touched in this chapter. It is good to remember that there are lots of very specialized cases of both git fetch and git push usages.

9.1.1. Syntax

refspec is a string used to specify mapping between branches names in the source repository and their counterpart in the destination repository. It is used by the fetch and push commands.

> *refspec* consists of four parts +<**src**>:<**dst**>.
>
> - plus (+)
> - the source <src>
> - colon (:) separating the source from the destination
> - the destination <dst>
>
> All parts are optional. Lack of colon means empty destination.

> Plus (+) demands to accept the changes normally rejected, (e.g. non-fast-forward).

Thus:

src is an abbreviation for src: — it means that the destination is empty,

:dst means that the source is empty.

Analogically, but with forcing the acceptation of the non-fast-forward changes:

+src empty destination,

+:dst empty source.

Even both source and destination can be empty. That is just colon alone (:) or colon preceded by plus (+:).

Using plus (+) allows e.g. to:

- Non-fast-forward modification of local branches by git fetch.
  Yes! git fetch can modify local branches, although you have to ask for it.
- Pushing non-fast-forward changes by git push.
  Accepting such changes by the remote repository is another matter. Most often it will automatically reject them. Unless you tell it explicitly (e.g. by the --force option) that you know what you are doing.

Most common refspec value is +refs/heads/*:refs/remotes/origin/*, but it can be complicated, e.g.:

- Asterisk * is pattern match in general.
- Negation ^ can be also used.

Specific refspec interpretation rules depend on the actual operation git fetch / git push and on the kind of the ref (tag/branch/commit/...).

9.1.2. *.git/config*

You can explicitly pass refspec to both fetch and push commands. You can also pass only a part (<src> or <dst>). Git searches the missing values in the configuration.

In the configuration of the remote repository — let's say origin — i.e. usually in the .git/config file, you can expect something like this:

```
[remote "origin"]
    url = https://github.com/git/git
    fetch = +refs/heads/*:refs/remotes/origin/*
```

but in general configuration looks like this:

```
[remote "<name>"]
        url = <URL>
        pushurl = <pushurl>
        push = <refspec>
        fetch = <refspec>
```

pushurl defaults to <URL>. Which means that by default Git should push to the same place it fetches from.

9.1.3. During fetching

In git fetch case, <src> and <dst> are seen from the remote repository point of view. It agrees with the direction of sending the data — from remote to local.

If you don't give the refspec at all, the value from the configuration is used to specify **what** should be fetched and **where** it should go. If you give the refspec with the empty <dst>, it is known **what** should be fetched (this what was specified by <src>). **Where** should the thing land up is established based on the configuration value.

Without giving <refspec>

Not giving <refspec> means, that during execution of:

```
git fetch [<remote>]
```

— assuming the standard value: +refs/heads/*:refs/remotes/<remote>/* in the configuration — Git:

- searches for the branches in the refs/heads/* in repository <remote>
- creates/modifies appropriate remote-tracking branches in refs/remotes/<remote>/* in the local repository.

With giving <refspec>

In the case of the command:

```
git fetch <remote> <branch>
```

the refspec from the configuration will be used only to establish what is the counterpart of branch <branch> in the local repository.

Examples

Let's take a closer look at this. The command above is a shorter version of the command (reminder: lack of colon means empty <dst>):

```
git fetch <remote> <branch>:
```

And it just means: deal yourself with the branch name in the local repository.
And more precisely:

- Fetch the value of <branch> from <remote>.
- Check where, according to the refspec from the configuration the corresponding remote-tracking branch should be found.
- Modify the remote-tracking branch or create it if needed.

While:

```
git fetch <remote> <remote-branch>:<local-branch>
```

does a little bit more. In addition, it modifies local branch `<local-branch>`.

Notice, that it is a way to update a branch without switching to it. I.e. if `feature` is the current branch, and for any reason you want to update branch `main`, you can do it in many ways, e.g.

```
git checkout main
git fetch
git merge
git checkout -
```

Probably, you will have to additionally execute `git stash`, `git stash pop` or something like that. Instead, you can execute:

```
git fetch <remote> main:main
```

If the change is non-fast-forward, a problem will arise:

```
 ! [rejected]          main      -> main  (non-fast-forward)
```

To force the change, you can add plus:

```
git fetch origin +main:main
```

and expect something like:

```
 + dff47f9d86...b23316302d main      -> main  (forced update)
```

The same effect you can achieve in a less direct way:

```
git fetch origin main ①
git branch -f main origin/main ②
```

① Modification of the remote-tracking branch.
② Modification of the tracking branch.
   Alright: `main` doesn't even have to track `origin/main`. The command just changes branch `main`

so that it points to the same commit as origin/main does.

9.1.4. During pushing

In git push case, <src> and <dst> are seen from the local repository point of view. It agrees with the direction of sending the data — from local to remote.

If you don't give refspec, the value from the configuration will be used. If this value has not been set (usually it hasn't!), the current branch will be pushed to the upstream. More precisely, behaviour depends on push.default setting, which defaults to simple.

The exact behaviour is complicated but in general:

- Empty <dst> means: establish appropriate names in remote based on <src>. Usually: the name in the remote repository is the same as its counterpart in the local repository.
- <src> can be any expression, <dst> has to be specified is this case.

Examples

Deleting a remote branch

```
git push <origin> :<branch>
```

It can be understood this way: Change branch <branch> in the remote repository so that it points to what is specified on the left side of colon. Which is nothing in this case. So delete the branch.

Move master one commit back

```
git push origin HEAD~:master
```

In general there can be any commit on the left hand side. *Non-fast-forward* requires forcing (**--force** option).

Pushing current branch to the specified remote repository

```
git push [-u | --set-upstream] <remote> HEAD
```

Git will find out the branch name itself.

9.2. *repository* — not only <remote>

In commands referencing to the remote repositories you can use:

Names of the remote repositories defined in the local repository.

In this book such possibility is the only one being used.

Specific URL forms.

Detailed description can be found in the documentation, see *Git URLs [https://git-scm.com/docs/git-fetch#_git_urls]*.

Names of the repositories defined outside the local repository.

Detailed description can be found in the documentation, see *remotes [https://git-scm.com/docs/git-fetch#_remotes]*.

Basic information about configuration of the remote repositories can be displayed by:

```
git remote -v
```

and exhausting about an individual <remote>:

```
git remote show <remote>
```

The second command looks into the remote repository to find out some information.

10. Reconciliation of changes

10.1. git checkout — creating a local branch from a remote-tracking one

git checkout command was described in the first part of the book (see *git checkout*). But the second part was needed to describe what's exactly happening during execution of:

```
git checkout <branch>
```

when name <branch> **doesn't exist**. When there is no such branch nor tag.

Notice, that this is a very common situation:

- someone creates branch <branch>,
- pushes it,
- someone else interested in this new branch executes commands:
  git fetch
  git checkout <branch>.

Git seeing, that neither branch <branch> nor tag <branch> exists, enumerates the remote-tracking branches. If <branch> identifies a branch in exactly one remote repository, let's say <remote>, Git executes:

```
git checkout -b <branch> --track <remote>/<branch>
```

So branch <branch> gets created. Moreover, it tracks <remote>/<branch> and initially points to the same commit as <remote>/<branch>.

In other words, the result is similar to:

```
git checkout -b <branch> <remote>/<branch>
git branch --set-upstream-to=<remote>/<branch>
```

Ok, more precisely:

```
git checkout -b <branch> <remote>/<branch>^{commit}
git branch --set-upstream-to=<remote>/<branch>
```

as:

```
git checkout -b <branch> <remote>/<branch>
```

sets up the upstream itself.

10.2. git rebase — default values of parameters

git rebase command was described in the first part of the book (see *Rebasing — transplanting branches*). But the second part was needed to fully describe git rebase's default parameters.

In the general form below all parameters are optional:

```
git rebase [-i] [--onto <new-base>] [<upstream> [<branch>]]
```

If you don't give any of them, the following values will be used:

```
git rebase --onto HEAD@{upstream} HEAD@{upstream} HEAD
```

For example, if `master` is the current branch:

```
git rebase
```

expands to:

```
git rebase --onto origin/master origin/master master
```

This command rebases the commits added to branch `master` locally onto `master` fetched from `origin`. So it is integration of the local development with what has been developed remotely.

> By default, the values of the command:
>
> ```
> git rebase [-i] [--onto <new-base>] [<upstream> [<branch>]]
> ```
>
> are:
>
> | | |
> |---|---|
> | `<branch>` | HEAD, more precisely the current branch. |
> | `<upstream>` | Upstream of branch `<branch>`. |
> | `<new-base>` | The value of the `<upstream>` parameter
In particular, if parameter `<upstream>` is not given explicitly, `<new-base>` defaults to the upstream of branch `<branch>`. |

10.3. Configuration of using rebase instead of merge as default

Merge is default method used for reconciliation of the changes (during `git pull`). If you want to use rebase instead just once, you can do this:

```
git pull --rebase
```

Of course, you can do it in two steps as well:

```
git fetch
git rebase
```

If you want to always use rebase for a specific branch, configuring that branch can be useful:

```
git config branch.<branch>.rebase true
```

Moreover, the repository can be configured like this:

```
git config branch.autosetuprebase always
```

Then, after executing `git checkout <branch>` (on a new `<branch>` in the repository), `git config branch.<branch>.rebase true` will be executed automatically. If you want this behaviour to be default, you can set it globally:

```
git config --global branch.autosetuprebase always
```

You can also set up Git to use rebase as the default:

```
git config --global pull.rebase true
```

Conclusion

Some information contained in this book is not necessarily exact. This is because Git allows to configure the individual commands and options to a big extent. E.g. using `clone.defaultRemoteName` option one can change the default name of remote repository (`origin`).

Default configuration allows to make everyday work comfortable and the book assumes the default configuration.

Writing a book that is exact, exhausting and easy to understand appears to be impossible. I just wanted to give the reader solid foundation for using and understanding Git on the level just enough for a programmer. And a good starting point for those who want more. As it stands in documentation:

> After you mastered the basic concepts, you can come back to this page to learn what commands Git offers.
>
> — man git

In particular the reader might want to learn about topics not described in this book. E.g.:

- **Submodules** [https://git-scm.com/docs/gitmodules].
- **Attributes** [https://git-scm.com/docs/gitattributes]. E.g. in case of having to manage the end of line (Linux vs Windows).
- Using many working trees: **git worktree** [https://git-scm.com/docs/git-worktree].

- Rewriting branches massively: ***git filter-branch*** [https://git-scm.com/docs/git-filter-branch].
- Built-in graphical tools: **gitk**.
- Clearing the working tree: ***git clean*** [https://git-scm.com/docs/git-clean].
- Adding notes: ***git notes*** [https://git-scm.com/docs/git-notes].
- Commands still marked as experimental in the documentation, and not used in this book in favour of old, good git checkout, git reset, git branch.
  - ***git restore*** [https://git-scm.com/docs/git-restore] — restoring files in working tree (from version 2.25.0).
  - ***git switch*** [https://git-scm.com/docs/git-switch] — switching between branches (from version 2.27.0).

And many more ...

Thank you!

www.ingramcontent.com/pod-product-compliance
Lightning Source LLC
LaVergne TN
LVHW081530050326
832903LV00025B/1718